Roots, shoots & leaves

BERNADETTE LE ROUX

Cooking with Vegetables

Photography by Russel Wasserfall

SUNBIRD PUBLISHERS

To my boys, Matt and Liam

"I hope there will be time to think vegetables handsome and to enjoy their looks. I hope there will be time for fun – to chat to seed potatoes reminding them how Sir John Hawkins, that old pirate, who took them from South America to Ireland, had a great-granddaughter who married a Palmer boy. 'Old friends,' you shall say, 'remember, this is a family do. Get going'. I hope that there will be time to get a pretty visitor to stroke a basil leaf (it loves a fair face); time not only to water lettuces, but to remember the Greek philosopher, Aristoxenus, who treated his lettuces with wine."

Eve Palmer, *Under the Olive: A Book of Garden Pleasures*

Contents

Foreword

I have always admired Bern's first cookbook *Prickly Pears & Pomegranates*, and I was lucky enough to work with her on my own cookbook *Reuben Cooks Local*. Bern shares with me a love of fresh produce and has a real passion for all that is local and truly *lekker*, as is evident on every page of her beautiful new book, *Roots, Shoots & Leaves*. And what an amazing piece of work it is once again. The ideas and recipes are fresh and original, and the illustrations and photography complement the text perfectly.

Roots, Shoots & Leaves is the culmination of Bern's mission to seek out long-forgotten produce and so it is fitting that the pages are filled with beautiful vegetables – some that we know well, and some that we have only heard about. The food is delicious and the colours vibrant; it's one of those books that will make you want to get cooking right away. Apart from the recipes, there is also interesting information and useful tips on the unusual vegetables that are used in her dishes – yet another testament to the author's quest to unearth and to share.

This book is clever, yet simple, and the easy-to-prepare recipes will be a firm favourite with foodies and amateur cooks alike.

I can't wait for it to find a place on my bookshelf and table.

Reuben Riffel

Introduction

I have a deep-seated love of vegetables that stems from a childhood spent on a farm in the Great Karoo where summers were fierce with endless dusty days and hot, restless nights. One would think that nothing grows in the desert. But this couldn't be further from the truth. An underground spring fed a rambling vegetable garden and vast orchard that produced all manner of greens, from spinach and chard to delicate lettuces and fragrant herbs. Yes, there was meat – and lots of it. I come from a long line of sheep farmers producing the very best Karoo lamb, but mealtimes consisted of at least five side dishes: honey-roasted pumpkin, sticky and slightly blackened at the edges; the simplest plate of steamed green beans with a knob of melting butter; crimson orbs of beetroot under a velvet blanket of béchamel; freshly podded garden peas; baby gems with a whisper of nutmeg; rounds of aubergine dusted in flour and shallow-fried until golden and crisp.

Even though the side dish still holds pride of place at any mealtime, vegetables have become stars in their own right and are no longer simply seen as an accompaniment. Consider a delicate twice-baked cauliflower soufflé with sharp cheese and snipped chives as a starter; steamed asparagus in a light and fluffy crêpe with scrambled eggs and Hollandaise for brunch; a warming bowl of pasta with tenderstem broccoli tips, gorgonzola and walnuts on a cold winter's night.

With an ever-increasing number of people caring about where the food on their plate comes from, there's the growing trend to eat more vegetables and even to grow your own. I'm not a vegetarian by any means. But it's become too easy in this busy life to grill a piece of meat, toss a salad and call it supper. The point of this book is to get more creative with meatless menus and to try more unusual varieties of vegetables – even if it means you have to grow your own. It doesn't have to be complicated, but using the freshest ingredients you can find makes all the difference.

In these pages you'll find recipes that honour a host of vegetables from the humble spud to the more forgotten varieties such as salsify and celeriac, as well as best-loved greens such as spring asparagus, globe artichokes and tender baby spinach. This is a book for people who are passionate about produce – whether you're a vegetarian or not. A book that celebrates vegetables.

A Note on Heirlooms

Why do I love heirloom vegetables? What is it that attracts me to them? For a start, it's the rich, romantic history inevitably attached to these ancient varieties. By definition, a true heirloom is one that has been open-pollinated (by bees or the wind), nurtured and handed down from one family member to another. Mostly, through this long line of private exchange, there is a good story attached. And I love a good story. I once came across an old gentleman from the Transkei who was growing the long-forgotten South African variety of Transkei Flint Corn, which was thought to have died out. Thanks to him – and his ancestors, who'd been saving the seeds year after year for replanting – it is still with us today.

I've always been drawn to the gnarled and knobbly shapes of these ancient varietals with their quirky names – Box Car Willy tomatoes, Purple Dragon carrots, Painted Lady beans – and all the unusual colours. Who knew that once upon a time carrots were purple? Long before the Dutch started mass-producing carrots and developing strains that were orange (to suit the nation's favourite colour), carrots were long and thin – and purple! And before mass production, vegetables tasted the way they were meant to taste – full of flavour, with vibrant colours, interesting shapes and superior texture.

The definition of an heirloom vegetable is hotly debated. There are those who say the cultivar must be over 100 years old, others claim over 50 and some prefer the date of 1945, which marks the end of World War II and the beginning of widespread hybridisation by producers and seed companies – and hence the steady decline of heirloom varieties. Hybrid varieties have been developed to make vegetable farming commercially viable. Unlike heirlooms, hybrids generally have a longer shelf life, uniform colour and shape (making packaging and transportation easier), bigger fruit and early maturation, all of which make sound commercial sense. Heirlooms, however, are non-hybrid vegetables grown from non-commercial seed. And it's thanks to seed savers and home gardeners all over the world that we still have access to these gems today.

To save the true seed, it's important to bag at least one plant from every crop, to prevent cross-pollination. This means covering the strongest, healthiest plant from every crop before it goes to seed (brown paper packets work like a charm), saving the seeds from that plant, and then replanting the following season, and so on, and so on. It takes serious commitment, passion and dedication to secure an heirloom varietal's existence.

The Irish Potato Famine is a very good example of why heirlooms are important. Unfortunately, when food supply is dependent on a single variety or hybrid, it becomes vulnerable to specific pests and diseases. The Potato Famine was caused by

OPPOSITE: *Turks Turban pumpkin*

11

the overuse of a single line of seed potato, the Lumper – a poor-quality spud that was among the worst-tasting, but had a higher per-acre yield than any other variety, making it extremely commercially viable for farmers. As it turned out, the Lumper was highly susceptible to a disease known as 'late blight', which wiped out entire harvests. The famine that resulted led to the loss of 25 per cent of Ireland's population.

World-renowned plant collector Jack Harlan once said, 'The line between abundance and disaster is becoming thinner and thinner, and the public is unaware and unconcerned. Must we wait for disaster to be real before we are heard? Will people listen only after it is too late?' Growers of heirloom vegetables (which are naturally more pest-resistant) preserve and increase the genetic diversity of our food supply, decreasing the chance of disaster. Heirlooms also taste better due to the fact that they have been selected for flavour and hardiness, not for regular appearance and thick skin (which ensures less damage during handling and transporting).

For me, the great attraction of growing heirloom vegetables is discovering the joy in searching for the more unusual varieties that I am not able to buy at the supermarket but that I can plant at home. It may involve trawling internet sites, visiting farmer's markets, discovering new seed suppliers and thumbing through vegetable catalogues – but therein lies the fun and the beauty.

Over the years I have encountered many passionate growers and collectors who have been a constant source of inspiration to me in my journey to discovering forgotten vegetables. Here are some of my favourite sites where I order seeds for my garden online:

~ Jason Snell of The Drift Farm in Napier, *www.thedrift.co.za* is a wealth of information on heirlooms. For information, or to buy seed, visit the website.
~ Mahlathini Organics, *www.mahlathinorganics/seed-catalog* has an extensive list of seeds available to order.
~ *www.livingseeds.co.za* is an excellent source for heirloom seeds. Order online and they arrive in beautiful seed packs of recycled paper.
~ *www.organicseeds.co.za* is another great site for ordering seed packs.
~ *www.janesdeliciousgarden* has an excellent directory of contacts for ordering seeds and discovering heirlooms.
~ Shannon Draper at *www.thegravelgarden.com* is a passionate producer of heirlooms and supplier of rare seeds.
~ *www.soughtafterseedlings.co.za* is the African distributor of Italian seeds handed down from the Franchi family in Bergamo.
~ Steve Botha, best known as the Magic Man, grows a huge variety of heirloom and organic vegetables at his farm in Porterville. For stockists, call Magic Herbs on 022 931 3209.

OPPOSITE: *Purple Dragon carrots*

CHAPTER I

Roots, Tubers & Bulbs

Come winter and thoughts immediately turn to comfort food – slow braises, warming casseroles and hearty soups for cold winter's evenings. There is an inherent association between slow cooking and root vegetables. How apt then that these vegetables all grow beneath the dark, cold earth. Today, the shapes, colours and flavours of these hidden treasures are highly varied and cultivated – some may even say sophisticated – versions of their ancestors. Thousands of years ago carrots were purple and potatoes pink. Then there are the forgotten vegetables like salsify, scorzonera and celeriac. Let's not forget these primitive vegetables that sustained generations, not just for nourishment, but for flavour too. A silky soup of celeriac with the crunch of toasted almonds; salsify soldiers lying beneath a blanket of bubbling béchamel; crisp, shaved fennel bulb in a salad of cress and blood orange – these are just some of the methods of honouring these ancient vegetables.

BEETROOT

Autumn is the best time for young beets, which are sweet and earthy roasted with a glug of olive oil or a spoonful of butter. Best-known varieties of beetroot are crimson purple in colour, but it's the Victorian white and golden beets, which are more rounded in shape, that have the advantage of not bleeding. The most fascinating of all is the candy-striped Chioggia heirloom, which cooks to a pale shade of pink. Raw baby beets are delicious finely sliced into slaws or scattered over winter leaves; in the colder months their mature counterparts are unmatched slowly baked in a hot oven, pickled in vinegar or roasted and served with rounds of silky goat's cheese.

CARROTS

It's hard to believe that centuries ago carrots were purple and stick-thin. An ancient vegetable, thought to have originated in Afghanistan, it's been modified and cultivated into the golden root we know it as today. Purple Dragon, a popular heirloom variety, is possibly the most striking of them all with its golden flesh coated in carmine-coloured skin (*see* A Note on Heirlooms on page 11). De Djerba is just as bold in shades of black, umber and violet. Carrots are good simply piled up on a plate with melting butter and a hint of orange zest; grated with toasted seeds, cumin and fresh coriander; blended into a silky soup with ginger and honey; or simply sautéed to form the backbone of a winter vegetable stew.

CELERIAC

With its gnarled and knobbly skin, it's hard to imagine the clean, crisp flesh hidden beneath the rough exterior. But once you've cleaned and peeled it, celeriac presents a world of opportunities – roasted and mashed together with sweet potato it makes for a happy alternative to the usual mashed potato. Or shave it and serve in a raw salad with a vinegary, robust dressing. But best of all is to sauté and then simmer it with new season's potatoes and blend into a soup scattered with toasted almonds. It is vegetables such as these that are slowly finding their way back into the modern-day kitchen.

FENNEL BULB

My great-aunt, Eve Palmer, enjoyed Elizabeth David-inspired recipes using fennel bulbs, which her grandmother (and my great-grandmother) grew abundantly in the Karoo. In those days, a popular way of preparing them would be to cook the bulbs in chicken stock until tender, place in a dish and cover with breadcrumbs toasted in butter, before warming through in the oven. But the steely crispness of raw, shaved fennel is just as good in a salad. It may resemble the bulbous head of celery in some ways, but the sharp, aniseed flavour is unmistakably its own. Tossed with blood orange segments and toasted almonds it makes for a zesty salad on a warm winter's day.

GARLIC

Garlic provides aroma, depth and warmth to any dish. It had been used in Mediterranean cooking long before the Romans made it a regular part of the soldier's diet. Use it as a base in casseroles, soups and sauces – but be sure not to burn it, as it will turn bitter. Best of all is to roast a whole head of garlic, unpeeled, until the edges catch and blacken slightly – this is when you know it's ready to squeeze the melting flesh onto a slice of warm crusty bread. (Garlic bread takes on a whole new meaning if you wrap the bulbs in foil, place on the braai, and eat it this way.)

HORSERADISH

Horseradish has to be one of the most underrated of all roots. And I'm not talking about the pulp you'll find in jars on supermarket shelves. Unearthed, scrubbed and freshly grated (you'll need gloves and glasses, so probably best to use a food processor), it can be added to vinaigrettes to dress Asian-inspired salads, stirred into crème fraîche and dolloped onto hot baked potatoes with a snip of chives, or pickled and bottled for later use. The piquant zing of fresh horseradish is addictive and pops and prickles on the palate – making you go back for more every time.

JERUSALEM ARTICHOKES

There is nothing on earth like a Jerusalem artichoke. It is neither an artichoke nor is it from Jerusalem – the faint resemblance in the flavour of its cream-coloured flesh and that of the globe artichoke must have earned it part of its name. Both earthy and delicately sweet, the flesh beneath its gnarled exterior is a luxurious accompaniment when braised in wine with garlic and onions. Roasted and stirred into a risotto with salted butter and Parmesan it makes for a warming, elegant main course when autumn is just beginning to wind down into winter and there's a decided chill in the air.

ONION

The backbone of many a dish, the humble onion is a star in its own right. There are countless types, varying in sweetness from the popular red onion to the sweet Spanish variety and the better-known yellow onion. As a general rule of thumb, violet-tinged and white onions are milder than their yellow counterparts, which are the most pungent. Slow braising and baking will mellow even the most powerful of bulbs.

PARSNIPS

If you've ever put your nose up close to a freshly unearthed parsnip, you will have noticed a decidedly fruity scent, which is no surprise really when you taste the sweet ivory flesh beneath the wiry exterior. Fluffy farm butter, rich cream and warming spices all marry well with parsnips, whether roasted, mashed, stewed or fried. Parsnips give a new dimension to soups and stews as they add their own distinctive sweetness to dishes. A stand-by winter recipe, which you will find in these pages, is parsnips in a spicy root vegetable casserole with all the lovely warming elements of North African cooking.

POTATOES

The variety and true beauty of the potato has long been forgotten due to the bags of one-dimensional 'BP' (baking potato) supermarket spuds that have occupied shelves for decades. Thankfully the ancient heirloom varieties are beginning to make a comeback. There's the Odem with its violet-blue skin; firm, waxy Roseval celebrated for its nutty flavour; pale cerise Kerr's Pink; and the russet-skinned Golden Wonder, a favourite for roasting and frying. 'Fluffy' or 'floury' varieties are good for baking, mashing and roasting; and 'waxy' potatoes, which keep their shape, are best for salads and golden gratins.

RADISH

Radishes present themselves in all their peppery splendour within a couple of weeks of planting. Best eaten when young and crisp, they enhance the flavour of almost any salad and most Asian-inspired dishes. A radish dipped into soft butter with a sprinkling of coarse salt is one of life's simple pleasures. Heirloom Easter Egg radishes are aptly named for their size and variance in colour; whereas the White Icicle is a long, broad root compared to the little red orbs we're used to. A member of the mustard family, radishes should be eaten raw whilst the sweet heat is at its best and brings any dish to life.

SALSIFY

A strange old thing, salsify. The milky-white flesh possesses a delicate flavour likened to asparagus and artichokes, but without the sweetness of a parsnip. The long, slender roots of salsify and scorzonera (black-skinned salsify) are harvested in late autumn and are among the few vegetables that benefit from boiling for long periods of time. Salsify was just made to lie under a blanket of rich, gratinéed béchamel, bubbling and golden. It reminds me of a childhood in the Karoo, where my grandfather grew heaps of it and loved it best with melted butter, a squeeze of lemon juice and a sprinkling of parsley.

Sweet potato

There is no simpler pleasure than a sweet potato baked in the oven until the skin is oozing with caramel and bursting open, a knob of butter melting into the pale yellow flesh. Completely unrelated to the humble spud, the sweet potato caramelises beautifully when roasted. Both the red- and orange-skinned varieties can be used in much the same way as you would a potato: steamed or boiled and then mashed with butter and cream; drizzled with oil and roasted until golden; deep-fried until crispy on the outside and fluffy within; or simply baked and served as a meal in itself.

Turnips

There's really only one way to eat turnips, and that's when they're young – so small that you can hold the pale, lilac-tinged orbs (no bigger than a golf ball) in the palm of your hand. You won't even need to peel them. Toss in olive oil and roast with a generous seasoning of salt; drop into boiling salted water until tender then gloss the skins with a drizzle of honey and pan-fry until caramelised; or roast until golden and add to a warm vegetable salad. One of my all-time favourite recipes is whole baby turnips roasted with the skins on and dressed in a warm caper vinaigrette.

Chilled Beet and Apple Soup

Don't even think about making this soup unless you have the season's very first beets at hand. They need to be sweet, earthy and smooth. The addition of apple adds a tartness, which makes it perfect served chilled on a warm autumn's day. You could substitute the crème fraîche with Bulgarian yoghurt for a healthier option – and it's just as tasty.

1 onion, finely sliced
1 carrot, finely diced
2 sticks celery, finely sliced
1 Tbs (30 g) butter
1 clove garlic, crushed
750 g young beets, trimmed and
  diced
2 Granny Smith apples
4 cups (1 litre) vegetable stock,
  preferably homemade
crème fraîche, to serve
snipped chives, to garnish

SERVES 4–6

Slowly sauté the onion, carrot and celery in the butter until the onion is translucent, but not yet brown. Add the garlic and sauté for a minute or two, taking care not to burn the garlic as it will turn bitter and spoil the entire dish.

Add the beetroot and apple and sweat for 2 minutes before pouring in just enough stock to cover, about 1 litre. Bring to the boil, and then simmer until the beetroot is tender, about 20 minutes. Leave to cool, then purée.

For a silky smooth version, push through a sieve at this stage. It may seem like a lot of trouble, but the result is well worth the effort. Season and chill.

Serve with a dollop of crème fraîche and a flourish of snipped chives.

Carrot and Red Lentil Soup with Coriander

Carrot and coriander is a classic combination. If you can find fresh coriander with the roots intact, be sure to chop the roots and stems finely and sauté them with the onion in the first stages of the recipe to add depth of flavour. The addition of red lentils makes for a wholesome meal-in-one kind of soup, which is perfect with crusty French bread.

1 onion, finely chopped
roots and stems of 1 bunch of
   fresh coriander, finely chopped
   (optional)
1 Tbs (30 g) butter
1 Tbs (15 ml) olive oil
4 medium to large carrots, diced
2 cloves garlic, finely chopped
1 cup (200 g) red lentils
3 cups (750 ml) vegetable stock,
   preferably homemade
150 g fresh coriander leaves, finely
   chopped
salt and black pepper, to taste
cream (optional)

SERVES 4 – 6

Sauté the onion and coriander roots and stems (if using) in the butter and oil until the onion is translucent but not yet brown.

Add the carrots and garlic, and sauté for another 3 minutes, allowing the flavours to develop. Add the lentils and stock, bring to the boil, then simmer for about 35 minutes or until the lentils are soft. Add more stock or water if necessary.

Add the fresh coriander leaves and season to taste. I like to blend this soup very quickly so that it's not completely smooth and maintains a slightly coarse texture.

To serve, top with fresh coriander and a swirl of cream.

Celeriac and Potato Soup with Toasted Almonds

This is a posh version of vichyssoise or cold potato and leek soup. The addition of parsley just before the end of the cooking time makes the flavours sing.

1 onion, finely sliced
2 medium-sized leeks, finely sliced
1 Tbs (30 g) butter
1 Tbs (15 ml) olive oil
1 whole celeriac root, peeled, cubed
4 large potatoes, cubed
4 cups (1 litre) vegetable stock,
  preferably homemade
½ cup (60 ml) parsley, finely
  chopped
salt and black pepper, to taste
½ cup (75 g) raw almond flakes,
  toasted

SERVES 4–6

Gently sauté the onion and leeks in the butter and olive oil, until translucent, but not brown.

Add the celeriac and potatoes, and sweat for a couple of minutes to develop the flavours.

Add enough stock to just cover the vegetables, about 1 litre, bring to the boil and simmer until the vegetables are tender, about 20 to 25 minutes. Add the parsley when the vegetables are just about soft. Season and blend until smooth.

Serve hot or cold, garnished with the toasted almonds scattered on top.

OVERLEAF: *Celeriac*

Asian Noodle Salad with Radishes and Pickled Ginger

This is a Café Roux favourite, and one you will always find on the menu in various guises. The dressing is completely moreish and can also be used as a marinade or a sauce, which is very good with eggs.

THE SALAD
400 g Chinese egg noodles
4 radishes, finely sliced
2 oranges, peeled and segmented
1 red pepper, diced
2 large handfuls rocket, baby
  spinach or Asian greens
¼ cup pickled ginger
fresh coriander, to garnish

HONEY AND SOY DRESSING
3 Tbs (45 ml) soy sauce
3 Tbs (45 ml) freshly squeezed lime
  or lemon juice
dash Worcester sauce
1 clove garlic, finely chopped
3 cm fresh ginger, grated
1 Tbs (15 ml) raw honey
¾ cup (190 ml) extra virgin olive oil
½ cup fresh coriander, finely chopped
½ red chilli, deseeded, finely chopped

SERVES 4

Cook the noodles according to the packet instructions. Set aside to cool slightly (this is a salad that can be served warm or cold, but you don't want to toss in the salad ingredients while the noodles are still piping hot).

To make the dressing, whisk all the ingredients together, or shake vigorously in a jar. Taste and adjust flavours if necessary.

Once the noodles have cooled, toss in the rest of the salad ingredients, dress and serve topped with coriander.

Roast Beetroot Salad with Goat's Cheese

I like to roast whole unpeeled beets wrapped in foil, as the juices are retained and the skin becomes meltingly soft, lending a distinct earthiness to the dish. There's no better marriage than goat's cheese and beetroot with toasted seeds to add crunch.

THE SALAD

5 medium-sized beetroots, scrubbed, unpeeled
sea salt
freshly ground black pepper
olive oil, for roasting
½ cup (75 g) seeds, for toasting (I like to use sunflower and pumpkin seeds)
300 g baby leaves
1 handful beet shoots (optional)
1 log chevin goat's cheese

HONEY AND GINGER DRESSING

3 Tbs (45 ml) balsamic vinegar
3 Tbs (45 ml) freshly squeezed lemon juice
1 clove garlic, finely chopped
3 cm fresh ginger, grated
1 Tbs (15 ml) raw honey
¾ cup (180 ml) extra virgin olive oil

SERVES 6

Season the beets, drizzle with olive oil and wrap all together in a single foil parcel. Roast in a preheated oven at 200 °C for about an hour, or until soft.

While the beets are roasting, make your salad dressing and toast the seeds. I like to use a mixture of pumpkin seeds and sunflower seeds. Place the seeds in a dry saucepan and toast over a medium heat, shaking the pan regularly, until golden. (Watch them closely so that they don't burn.)

To make the dressing, whisk all the ingredients together, or shake vigorously in a jar. Taste and adjust flavours if necessary. Set aside until you are ready to serve.

Once your beets are ready, open the parcel and leave until cool enough to handle. Slice into quarters.

On a platter, or in six individual salad bowls, scatter your baby leaves and beet shoots and gently place the beetroot in and around the leaves, taking care not to 'stain' the leaves and shoots. Dot the goat's cheese over the salad and sprinkle over the toasted seeds. Dress the salad only once you are ready to serve.

Salad of Asian Greens with Fresh Horseradish Dressing

This is a recipe I discovered through a good friend. It's evolved somewhat over time, as it's one I keep coming back to. Specific amounts of greens and sliced vegetables haven't been given as you can use as much or as little of each as you please. You can add your own Asian-inspired favourites such as snow peas or baby corn. This is a great salad for serving a crowd. Note that you can substitute the horseradish in the dressing with hot English mustard.

THE SALAD
baby tatsoi leaves
red cabbage, shredded
watercress
mange tout, finely sliced
carrot, finely julienned or sliced
  with a mandolin shaver
red pepper, finely sliced
bean sprouts
fresh coriander (optional)
radishes, finely sliced
cashew nuts
sesame seeds
ramen or 2-minute noodles, crushed

HORSERADISH DRESSING
6 Tbs (90 ml) rice vinegar
2 Tbs (30 ml) soy sauce
3 cm fresh ginger, finely grated
3 cm horseradish, finely grated (you
  can substitute with 2 teaspoons
  hot English mustard)
1 clove garlic, finely diced or grated
2 tsp (10 ml) raw honey
½ cup (125 ml) sunflower oil

MAKE AS MUCH AS YOU LIKE

Toss all the salad ingredients (except for the nuts, seeds and noodles) together in a large bowl.

Preheat your oven to 190 °C. Place the cashew nuts, sesame seeds and crushed noodles on a baking tray, and toast in the oven until golden brown and crispy; about 7 to 10 minutes. (Watch closely as they burn very easily and quickly if left unattended!)

For the dressing, whisk all the ingredients together, or shake vigorously in a jar. Taste and adjust flavours if necessary.

To serve, top the salad with the toasted nuts, seeds and noodles. Only dress the salad just before serving or your toasted ingredients will turn soggy.

Moroccan Salad of Raw Carrots, Beetroot and Dates

The addition of Purple Dragon heirloom carrots makes for a vibrant, striking dish. Wafer-thin strips of carrot add to the visual appeal, so don't be afraid to use a mandolin slicer. Equal amounts of lemon juice and extra virgin olive oil make for a surprisingly refreshing dressing, counter-balanced with the warmth of toasted and pounded cumin seeds and chopped dates.

MOROCCAN SALAD

6 carrots, cut into sticks (I like to use a mix of orange and Purple Dragon carrots)

4 medium beetroots, cut into sticks

1 handful of fresh coriander leaves, roughly chopped

½ cup (75 g) sunflower seeds

6–8 dates, pitted and finely chopped

CUMIN DRESSING

¼ cup (60 ml) extra virgin olive oil

¼ cup (60 ml) freshly squeezed lemon juice

2 tsp (10 ml) cumin seeds, toasted and pounded in a pestle and mortar

salt and pepper, to taste

1 tsp (5 ml) raw honey

SERVES 6 AS A SIDE DISH

Mix all the salad ingredients together in a large bowl and toss gently.

For the dressing, mix all the ingredients together and whisk to combine. Dress the salad only once you are ready to serve.

OVERLEAF: *Amarillo carrots*

A Salad of Fennel, Blood Orange and Toasted Almonds

The distinct aniseed flavour of the raw fennel marries well with the sharp, sweet blood orange and the crunch of toasted almonds. A cleansing, refreshing salad that will liven up any meal.

THE SALAD
2 fennel bulbs
4 blood oranges, segmented,
 membrane removed
300 g baby leaves
½ cup flaked almonds, toasted
fennel fronds, to garnish

LEMON DRESSING
3 Tbs (45 ml) freshly squeezed
 lemon juice
6 Tbs (90 ml) extra virgin olive oil
salt and black pepper, to taste

SERVES 6

Slice the fennel into wafer-thin slices so that you can almost see through them. Toss in a large bowl together with the blood orange segments and leaves, then either place on a large platter for sharing, or in six individual salad bowls.

For the dressing, whisk together all the ingredients until combined.

When you are ready to serve, dress the salad, then sprinkle over the toasted almonds and dot some fennel fronds around and about.

Two Ways with Scorzonera

For these two recipes, try to use young scorzonera, which saves you having to peel and scrape them. You could use salsify or a combination of the two vegetables together. Both of these dishes made regular appearances on our Karoo farm table when my grandfather was still alive – he loved salsify almost as much as he loved fudge!

FIRST WAY
10–12 scorzonera
3 Tbs (90 g) butter
juice of 1 lemon
parsley, finely chopped,
  for garnishing
salt
freshly ground black pepper

Clean the scorzonera by scrubbing with a brush. Cook in boiling salted water for about 30 minutes, or until tender. Now rub off the skins – they should come off easily.

Melt the butter and stir in the lemon juice. Adjust to taste. Pour the lemon butter over the scorzonera (be generous) and add a good sprinkling of finely chopped fresh parsley. Season well and serve.

SECOND WAY
10–12 scorzonera
olive oil
knob of butter
salt
freshly ground black pepper

For the second dish, scrub the scorzonera clean with a brush and place in a roasting pan with a drizzle of olive oil and a knob of butter. Season and roast at 190 °C until golden. Serve hot.

EACH RECIPE SERVES 4
AS A SIDE DISH

Spicy Root Vegetable Casserole

This is a beautiful warming dish, perfect for a chilly winter's evening. The flavours are North African, making it just the right accompaniment to couscous with a knob of melted parsley butter.

1 onion, finely sliced
4 carrots, thickly sliced
2 Tbs (30 ml) olive oil
2 cloves garlic, finely sliced
3 cm fresh ginger, grated
1 tsp (5 ml) ground turmeric
2 tsp (10 ml) ground cumin
1 dried bird's eye chilli, finely sliced
2 medium sweet potatoes, cubed
2 medium potatoes, cubed
2 parsnips, sliced into chunks
1 small butternut, deseeded and
  cubed
1 can (410 g) peeled, diced tomatoes
2 sticks cinnamon
2 bay leaves
2 cups (500 ml) vegetable stock,
  preferably homemade
1 can (400 ml) coconut milk
fresh mint, for garnishing

SERVES 6

Sauté the onion and carrots in the olive oil until the onion is translucent but not brown. Add the garlic and sauté for a further 2 minutes, stirring.

Add the ginger, spices and chilli and stir for about 2 minutes, until fragrant.

Add the root vegetables and the butternut, and sweat for a few minutes to develop the flavours. Stir in the tomatoes, cinnamon, bay leaves and stock.

Cover, and cook until the vegetables are soft; about 25 to 30 minutes.

Remove the lid and add the coconut milk. Bring to the boil, then remove from the heat. Garnish with fresh mint and serve with couscous.

Heirloom Potato Salad in Horseradish Mayonnaise

Of course you don't have to use heirloom potatoes for this recipe, although I do encourage you to think about the type of potato you choose instead of buying a bag of supermarket all-purpose 'BP'. It's best to use a waxy potato as the firmer flesh and high water content helps them keep their shape during cooking. A waxy potato can often be identified by its yellow flesh; floury varieties being much paler by comparison. The mayonnaise is a cheat's version, made using a hand blender. (Yes, it is possible and you'll never look back.)

8 waxy potatoes, peeled and cut into chunks
salt and white pepper, to taste

H O R S E R A D I S H   M A Y O N N A I S E
1 whole egg
1 Tbs (15 ml) lemon juice or white wine vinegar
1 tsp (5 ml) freshly grated horseradish
1 cup (250 ml) good-quality canola oil

S E R V E S   6   A S   A   S I D E   S A L A D

Boil the potatoes in salted water until cooked through. Drain and leave to cool while you make the mayonnaise.

Place all the mayonnaise ingredients in a clear glass container, big enough for a hand blender to fit in. Using your hand blender, whizz it all up until it thickens. It takes a mere matter of seconds.

This salad is best served warm. Pour the mayonnaise over the still warm (but not hot) potatoes, season and serve.

Jerusalem Artichoke Risotto

Slicing the Jerusalem artichokes thinly and pan-roasting them with the skins on results in a nutty flavour that adds depth to this rich and soothing risotto. Don't be shy with the Parmesan. The vermouth adds another dimension, but can be substituted with dry white wine.

4 Tbs (120 g) butter
4 Tbs (60 ml) oil
700 g Jerusalem artichokes,
  unpeeled, thinly sliced
salt and black pepper
4 cups (1 litre) warm vegetable
  stock, preferably homemade
1 onion, finely chopped
2 cups (400 g) risotto rice (Arborio
  is most readily available)
½ cup (125 ml) vermouth or dry
  white wine
zest of 1 whole lemon
knob of butter
1 very large handful good-quality
  grated Parmesan

Serves 6 – 8

Place 2 tablespoons each of the butter and oil in a large, heavy-bottomed saucepan. Add the Jerusalem artichokes, season and pan-fry on a low heat for about 15 to 20 minutes, giving the pan a shake every now and again. You want the artichokes to soften, but retain a slight crunch, as they will continue to cook when added to the risotto. Once they are golden, remove from the pan and set aside.

Make sure you have a pot of stock on a low heat on the stove before you start your risotto, as you want to add hot stock to the rice to prevent it from losing heat. In a heavy-bottomed pot, sauté the chopped onion in the remaining butter and oil until softened, but not golden.

Add the rice and sauté, stirring constantly, until the edges of the grains of rice become slightly translucent. Add the vermouth and cook until it has been absorbed by the rice.

Now start adding the stock, one ladle at a time, only adding the next ladle once the previous one has been completely absorbed by the rice. The whole process should take about 20 minutes, by which time the rice should have softened nicely. Now you can add the lemon zest and the Jerusalem artichokes.

Continue cooking and adding stock for about 5 minutes more to develop the flavours. Once the rice is completely cooked, remove from the heat, add the butter and Parmesan, give it a good stir and set aside, covered, for 2 minutes to allow the flavours to develop.

Serve immediately as risotto does not like to be reheated. Spoon onto six individual plates or bowls and serve with a wedge of Parmesan for grating extra cheese over the top.

Roast Baby Turnips with Warm Caper Vinaigrette

I like the texture and robust look of unpeeled, roast turnips – and their earthy flavour. Served with a warm caper vinaigrette, it's the sort of dish that can accompany just about any main and happily shares a harvest table of salads and vegetables.

1.5 kg whole baby turnips, unpeeled
olive oil, for roasting
salt and black pepper

Warm Caper Vinaigrette
2 Tbs (30 ml) capers
3 cloves garlic
juice of 1 lemon
½ cup (125 ml) olive oil
3 Tbs (90 g) butter, cubed

Serves 6 as a side dish

Scrub the turnips well, and place in a roasting dish. Season and drizzle generously with olive oil, and roast in a preheated oven at 190 °C for about 35 to 40 minutes, or until tender. Set aside, covered to keep warm, while you make the dressing.

Using a pestle and mortar, pound together the capers and garlic. Add the lemon juice.

In a saucepan, heat the olive oil until warm, add the caper mixture, then whisk in the butter, one cube at a time, until it is all emulsified.

Serve the vegetables, tossed in the warm caper dressing.

Onions on the Braai

There's nothing quite like a whole onion dotted with butter, wrapped in foil and left on the coals until meltingly soft and tender. It's a good idea to prepare at least one onion per person, as – once you've tasted it – it's not the sort of thing you'll want to share.

whole onions (allow 1 onion
 per person)
fresh thyme, chopped
butter, softened
salt and ground black pepper

MAKE AS MANY AS YOU LIKE

Cut the onions into quarters without cutting straight through, keeping the onion intact.

Mix the thyme into the butter. Push dots of thyme butter into the onion quarters, season generously and wrap in foil. Leave on the coals until meltingly soft and falling apart.

Pickled Horseradish

Horseradish grows prolifically in the Free State, which is where my mother's side of the family still farms today. This is one of my aunt Hannie's recipes, which ensures that a good crop of horseradish never goes to waste. You would use this pickle in the same way that you would a jar from the supermarket, but the flavour is far superior and worth the (minimal) effort.

2 cups (300 g) peeled and cubed
 horseradish
1 cup (250 ml) white vinegar

MAKE AS MUCH AS YOU LIKE

Pour the vinegar over the horseradish, then blend in a food processor. Place in sterilised jars, seal well and keep refrigerated.

TIP: Be sure to wear gloves when peeling and cubing horseradish – and don't be ashamed to wear some form of glasses either.

A Gratin of Salsify in Béchamel Sauce

This is an ancient recipe I dug up from one of my mother's '70s cookbooks. The sauce is similar to a white sauce, but has the added richness of egg and cream. I've adapted it to suit the more modern palate, but it remains delicious in all its richness. (Salsify is the paler version of scorzonera pictured on the next page.)

700 g salsify, peeled and cut into
  3 cm lengths
2 Tbs (30 ml) vinegar or lemon juice
salt

BÉCHAMEL SAUCE
2 cups (500 ml) milk
1 onion, quartered
2 bay leaves
1 Tbs (30 g) butter
1 Tbs (15 g) flour
salt, to taste
a pinch nutmeg
2 Tbs (30 ml) double cream
1 egg yolk
1 handful fresh breadcrumbs

SERVES 8 AS A SIDE DISH

While you are peeling the salsify, have a bowl of cold water ready containing the vinegar. Drop the peeled salsify into the vinegar solution – it will prevent it from turning black.

Boil the salsify in salted water for about 40 minutes, until just about cooked. Drain and keep warm in an oven-proof dish.

To make the béchamel, bring the milk, onion and bay leaves almost to the boil, until scalding, then remove from the heat.

Melt the butter in a saucepan and add the flour. Cook, stirring continuously, for about 2 minutes. Strain the milk and add to the saucepan. Stir until thickened. Season with salt and nutmeg, and stir in the cream and egg yolk.

Pour the sauce over the salsify, scatter over the breadcrumbs and bake in a preheated oven at 180 °C for about 35 minutes or until golden and bubbling.

OVERLEAF: *Scorzonera*

A Sticky Cake of Beetroot and Dark Chocolate

Somehow beetroot and dark chocolate were made to go together. Some may feel that this combination is gimmicky, but I disagree. Beetroot lends sweetness, which balances the bitterness of good dark chocolate. It's a beautiful-looking cake in an old-fashioned, wobbly kind of way — the centre may sink and crack ever so slightly when you remove it from the oven, but I think that adds to the charm.

200 g 70% dark chocolate, roughly
  chopped
250 g butter, cubed
1 cup (120 g) flour
1 tsp (5 ml) baking powder
3 Tbs (45 ml) cocoa powder
6 eggs, separated
250 g beetroot, boiled, peeled
  and puréed
1 cup (190 g) castor sugar

MAKES 1 LARGE CAKE

Melt the chocolate in a glass bowl set over a pot of simmering water. Drop the butter, one cube at a time, into the chocolate, stirring well until all the butter is incorporated. Turn off the heat.

In a large bowl, sift the flour, baking powder and cocoa powder together.

Remove the butter and chocolate mix from the heat, leave to cool slightly, then very quickly stir in the egg yolks (if the chocolate mix is too hot or you work too slowly, you'll end up with scrambled eggs). Fold in the beetroot purée.

Whisk the egg whites into stiff peaks, then fold in the sugar. Fold the egg whites into the chocolate mixture, then fold in the sifted dry ingredients.

Pour into a greased 22 cm-diameter cake tin and bake in a preheated oven at 160 °C for 40 minutes.

Allow to cool and serve with cream or mascarpone.

Moist Carrot Cake with Mascarpone Icing

This is my mother's recipe for carrot cake, which has done the rounds in the Karoo and beyond. The addition of pineapple makes it especially moist and the mascarpone icing is my own twist on an old faithful.

CARROT CAKE
2 ½ cups (300 g) cake flour,
   preferably stone-ground
2 tsp (10 ml) baking powder
1 ½ tsp (7 ml) bicarbonate of soda
1 Tbs (15 ml) mixed spice
1 tsp (5 ml) salt
1 ½ cups (375 g) castor sugar
1 ¼ cups (310 ml) oil
4 large eggs (room temperature)
2 cups grated carrots
1 can crushed pineapple, drained
½ cup (50 g) chopped pecan nuts
¼ cup (80 g) smooth apricot jam

MASCARPONE ICING
100 g butter
4 cups (500 g) icing sugar, sifted
1 tsp (5 ml) vanilla extract
1 tsp (5 ml) freshly squeezed lemon
   juice, or to taste
250 g mascarpone

MAKES 1 LARGE CAKE

For the carrot cake, sift all the dry ingredients, except for the sugar, twice into a large mixing bowl.

In a separate mixing bowl, using an electric cake mixer, beat the sugar, oil and eggs together at high speed until smooth (mix for about 3 minutes). Add the carrots, pineapple, nuts and apricot jam, and mix well. Fold in the dry ingredients in batches, using a spatula, until well combined.

Grease a 28 cm-diameter loose-bottomed springform or Bundt cake tin, and sprinkle lightly with fine, dry breadcrumbs. Pour the mixture into the cake tin and bake in a preheated oven at 180 °C for 45 minutes. Allow to cool in the tin for about 10 minutes before turning out onto a wire rack to cool.

For the icing, cream the butter and icing sugar using an electric beater, adding the sugar gradually, mixing well. Add vanilla extract, lemon juice and mascarpone (taking care not to beat it too much or it will turn watery). Place in the fridge for a few minutes to firm up. Ice the cake when cooled completely.

CHAPTER 2

Eat Your Greens

Most people, when they think about green vegetables, have the association of being scolded as children to 'Eat your greens!' But those were the days when cabbage was boiled until grey, green beans were limp and overcooked, and the only way to eat spinach was in a blanket of white sauce.

Thankfully, varieties and flavours have come a long way in the last decade. Once upon a time the only lettuce available was iceberg, and rocket was a rarity. Today we are spoilt for choice with micro greens, soft herbaceous salad varieties such as watercress and lamb's lettuce, purple-sprouting broccoli, and interesting heirlooms such as cavolo nero (black kale) and rainbow chard, which not only make for beautiful plates of food, but taste the way vegetables should taste – fresh and full of flavour.

Some of my favourite recipes feature greens: slow-braised cabbage with apple and cranberries; a crisp phyllo tart of young spinach and cheese; raw broccoli salad with toasted pine nuts, baby tomatoes and sweet vinaigrette; a silky soup of cauliflower with Parmesan crisps for dipping.

I was raised on greens. More out of lack of choice and supermarket treats than for wanting. And thanks to my great-aunt, the legendary author Eve Palmer, there is a pile of journals and manuscripts documenting a rich history of just about every vegetable ever grown on our Karoo family farm, Cranemere. We grew all manner of vegetables, but besides all the varieties available to us, salad greens have always been significant. My great-grandfather adored them, planting any kind that could stand the Karoo climate – he grew them in winter to prevent bolting from excessive summer heat. He would have lettuce for breakfast, crunching on iceberg while dreaming about sheep.

ASPARAGUS

One of the first spring vegetables to make it to the table are lively green spears of asparagus. The short season starts in late September and it's best to make the most of it while it lasts – cook till soft with the slightest crunch and dress in butter and lemon juice; serve in a salad of new potatoes with a salsa verde dressing; or use in tart fillings with handfuls of pecorino and egg custard. By the end of the six-week season the spears get fatter, paler and pricier and it's best to cut your losses and say goodbye – until the next year.

BROCCOLI

Broccoli, with its tight, cloud-like florets, is closely related to cauliflower and has been a favourite winter vegetable for generations. A raw salad of little florets tossed with toasted pine nuts and tomato has become a firm favourite in my kitchen. The long, slim stems of green- and purple-sprouting broccoli are now also widely available and are delicious steamed and served with heaps of butter and a whisper of lemon. Left unharvested, the tight flower buds develop into delicate yellow flowers, which are delicious sprinkled over salads. But a quick warming dish of sprouting broccoli with cream and Gorgonzola is hard to beat.

CABBAGE

Firm-headed cabbages – red, white or green – are widely available in winter and are at their best when tightly formed with crunchy, unblemished outer leaves. Cored and shredded, cabbage is good sautéed, boiled or served raw in salads and slaws. Red cabbage is unparalleled in flavour when left to braise in a shallow pool of vinegar with grated apple and cranberries until soft and tender – the cranberries offer a sweet, tart pop of flavour. Leafy cabbages need less cooking time than their firm-headed counterparts and the pale, crinkly leaves of Chinese cabbage – delicate and crisp by comparison – are delicious flash-fried in stir fries.

CAULIFLOWER

Early strains of cauliflower had heads no bigger than golf balls. Thankfully they have improved in size over the years. The curds or florets should be firm and pale without freckles or blemishes, making for beautiful clouds of white when steamed. A take on traditional cauliflower cheese is to steam a whole head of lime-green Romanesco and carefully ladle over the sauce so that glimpses of green peer out from below the white blanket of cheese. Romanesco, a magnificent heirloom with its florets turreted like a fairy castle, is sometimes available at select supermarkets and is very often found at bigger fresh produce markets. It's well worth buying purely as a thing of beauty.

CHARD

Swiss chard is not as refined as true spinach – in flavour or in texture – but it has its own place in the kitchen. The stems can be cooked with the leaves while the plant is young, but are best discarded as they thicken with age. The stems are known as 'chards' (which is where the plant gets its name) and come in all shades from ruby and ivory white to canary yellow and apricot. Bright Lights with its raspberry red, yellow and orange stalks is widely available from nurseries countrywide and is easy to grow. Rhubarb chard is more difficult to come by and not as hardy, but seeds can be ordered online (*see* A Note on Heirlooms on page 12).

COURGETTES

Courgettes are miniature marrows and range in colour from light to dark green and are sometimes yellow-striped. A freshly picked courgette is glossy with a clean-cut, slightly hairy stalk. Courgettes can be baked (with herbed breadcrumbs), stuffed (with rice, garlic, lemon and tomato), grated into potato rostis and fresh salads, or grilled on the braai or in the oven. The clean, fresh flavour is heightened with the addition of lemon, mint and chalky cheeses like sheep's pecorino. But if you're able to scratch the skin off a courgette with your fingernail, it's a sure sign that it's past its best and better left alone.

KALE

Kale looks as beautiful in a vase of water as it does in the garden. Elongated, plume-like leaves glisten in shades of blue-green and dusky emerald. Unfortunately it has a negative reputation due to the fact that it was one of the few vegetables that survived winter frosts and was therefore associated with poverty and famine; a 'hungry-gap' vegetable. But much depends on the variety. Black kale or cavolo nero (see page 50) is easy to grow and sometimes available at fresh produce markets. The bittersweet characteristics shine in a warming soup-stew of beans, garlic and Parmesan and its renowned disease-fighting abilities make it a grand choice for juicing with crisp, sweet apple and a hit of ginger. Curly-leafed kale can be treated in much the same was as cabbage, shredded, plunged into boiling water then sautéed in a pan of butter, melting garlic and a squeeze of lemon juice.

LEAVES

Growing up in South Africa the choice of salad leaves was limited to watery, crisp iceberg and little else. Rocket, mizuna and radicchio were unheard of, and it wasn't until the mid-nineties that loose-leafed and tightly spun varieties became available. There is something to enjoy all year round: soft, fresh summer varieties like lollo rosso and then the bitter winter leaves of chicory and endive. Imagine a tangle of sweet summer leaves tossed in the lightest of herb vinaigrettes; crisp stems of chicory served with a bowl of hummus for scooping; or a simple, perfect head of cos alongside a craggy-edged wedge of Parmesan.

MICRO LEAVES

Also known as micro greens, living greens and micro herbs, these are essentially vegetable and herb seedlings that are picked between six and 21 days old. Miniature versions of the adult plant, micro leaves are easy to grow at home, all year round, in recycled margarine tubs, yoghurt pots or plastic punnets. Ensure adequate drainage by skewering a couple of holes in the bottom, then fill up with seed compost or vermiculite. Most of the seeds can be sowed dry and stored on a windowsill in a warm room. My favourite micro leaves are sunflowers, snow peas or Chinese pea, Genovese basil, mustard leaves and beetroot. They are highly nutritious, packing a punch of flavour into salads or used as garnish.

SPINACH

Creamed spinach is the simplest dish and one that has stood the test of time. When prepared correctly, it is just as it was meant to be – dark, tangled leaves lying wilted beneath a blanket of cosy cream. And yet it is in such stark contrast to the squeaky fresh vibrance of young English spinach, which can just as easily be used in salads as in a warming pasta dish or a golden gratin. Easy to grow and easy to buy, fresh spinach needs mere seconds in the pan before it wilts down into a miniscule pile of green. There are some ingredients that were born to be with spinach: feta, mushrooms, garlic, lemon, butter, eggs. After all, what would Eggs Florentine or stuffed mushrooms be without spinach?

A Celebration of Garden Leaves

The dressing is key in this salad. Without it, all you're left with is a bowl of leaves. Feel free to use any of your favourite herbs in the salsa verde – soft herbs are best.

SALSA VERDE DRESSING
1 clove garlic
2 Tbs (30 ml) capers
2 handfuls parsley
1 handful basil
1 handful mint
1 Tbs (15 ml) Dijon mustard
½ cup (125 ml) red wine vinegar
sea salt and ground black pepper
1 cup (250 ml) extra virgin olive oil

THE SALAD
mixed leaves (I like to use rocket,
  baby gem, cos and red or green
  frilly lettuce)
1 handful pea shoots
8 nasturtium flowers

SERVES 4

For the dressing, place all the ingredients (except the olive oil) in a food processor, or use a hand blender, and blend until smooth – you could also use a pestle and mortar, but will have your work cut out for you. Add the olive oil and give it a good stir.

If you like a thinner dressing, add more red wine vinegar and olive oil at a ratio of 1:2 (vinegar to olive oil) until you are happy with the consistency.

To make the salad, toss all the leaves and pea shoots together in a large bowl and dress with the salsa verde. Garnish with the nasturtium flowers and serve.

Twice-baked Cheese and Courgette Soufflé

The beauty about these individual soufflés is that they can be prepared up to a day in advance. All it takes prior to serving is a quick second bake in the oven for fool-proof, perfect soufflés. The grated courgette lends flecks of green to a soothing, butter-yellow dish – a trick I learnt from Cape cooking doyenne Judy Badenhorst.

1 ½ cups (375 ml) milk
a pinch nutmeg
½ onion, peeled
2 Tbs (60 g) butter
2 Tbs (30 g) flour
1 cup (100 g) mature
  grated cheddar
5 courgettes, grated
5 eggs, separated
1 Tbs (15 ml) English mustard
1 ¼ cups (300 ml) cream
grated Parmesan cheese, for baking

SERVES 6

Heat the milk, nutmeg and onion in a saucepan. Remove from the heat just before boiling and leave to infuse. (Do not let the milk boil.)

Melt the butter in a separate saucepan, add the flour and cook, stirring, for about 2 minutes as if you were making a white sauce. Strain the milk and add to the roux of flour and butter, stirring well. Keep stirring until the sauce thickens. Remove from the heat, and stir in the cheddar, grated courgette, egg yolks and mustard. Set aside.

Whisk the egg whites to stiff peaks, then fold them into the sauce. Using a muffin tray, fill 6 greased hollows two-thirds full and stand in a *bain-marie* (use a deep-sided roasting dish and pour in enough boiling water to come halfway up the sides of the muffin tray). Place in a preheated oven at 170 °C and bake for 25 to 30 minutes.

Remove the muffin tray from the *bain-marie* and leave to cool. (Note that the soufflés can be prepared up to a day in advance up to this stage.)

When you are ready to serve, remove the soufflés from the muffin tray, place on individual deep-sided plates or in shallow bowls, pour a bit of cream (about 3 tablespoons each) over and around each soufflé and top with grated Parmesan. Bake in a preheated oven at 240 °C for 7 minutes until golden. Serve immediately.

Asparagus Crêpe with Scrambled Eggs

This is a classic breakfast item that appears on the Café Roux menu from time to time. You could substitute the asparagus with chopped spring onions when asparagus is out of season. It is especially good served for brunch.

1 bunch fresh green asparagus, gently steamed

THE CRÊPES
1 cup (120 g) flour
2 eggs
½ cup (125 ml) water
1 tsp (5 ml) sunflower oil
¼ cup (60 ml) chopped chives
1 ½ cups (375 ml) milk

THE HOLLANDAISE
1 egg
1 Tbs (15 ml) vinegar
1 Tbs (15 ml) lemon juice
500 g butter

THE SCRAMBLED EGGS
18 eggs
½ cup (125 ml) cream
snipped chives, to serve

SERVES 6

For the crêpes, place all the ingredients in a large mixing bowl and mix well using a balloon whisk until you get a smooth, lump-free batter. (Note that according to the quality of the flour, you may need slightly more or less water to get the right consistency.) In a crêpe pan, heat a bit of sunflower or vegetable oil and spoon in the mix, a ladleful at a time, cooking the crêpes on both sides until golden. Set aside until ready to use.

For the Hollandaise, place all the ingredients (except the butter) in a blender or food processor and blend well.

Heat the butter in the microwave until piping hot (it must be 'foaming' hot). With the motor of the blender running, slowly pour the hot butter into the blender in a slow and steady stream until the sauce begins to thicken. Once it has thickened you can pour in the rest of the butter and continue to blend until combined. (Do not put the Hollandaise in the fridge or it will separate!)

For the creamiest scrambled eggs, beat the eggs well with a balloon whisk and add the cream. Pour the mixture into a deep-sided saucepan and leave until the eggs start forming an omelette-like base, then stir gently. Leave. Then stir gently again. Keep stirring and leaving the eggs to settle until cooked to your liking.

I like to remove the eggs from the heat just before they are done to my liking (very soft!) as they continue to cook in the pan at a rapid rate. (Make sure the eggs are the last thing you do before serving.)

To serve, place a generous helping of scrambled eggs on one side of each crêpe, top with the asparagus, pour over a generous amount of Hollandaise and fold the rest of the crêpe over. Top with snipped chives.

Romanesco Cauliflower Cheese

Because Romanesco tends to be a bit smaller than regular cauliflower, I've used two for this dish. And it looks — and tastes — so delicious everybody will be coming back for more. Of course you could use white cauliflower, but the lime-green Romanesco with its fairy-castle turrets makes a striking alternative.

2 whole heads Romanesco
  cauliflower

MUSTARD CHEESE SAUCE
2 Tbs (60 g) butter
2 Tbs (30 g) flour
1 ½ cups (375 ml) milk
1 cup (100 g) grated mature cheddar
1 Tbs (15 ml) Dijon mustard
salt and pepper, to taste

SERVES 6 – 8 AS A SIDE DISH

Place the cauliflower upright in a steamer and steam until soft. Alternatively place in a deep pot with about 5 cm of water and simmer until cooked.

To make the mustard cheese sauce, melt the butter, stir in the flour and keep cooking and stirring for about 2 minutes. Pour in the milk, stirring continuously, until the sauce begins to thicken.

Remove from the heat, add the cheddar and stir until the cheese has melted. Stir in the mustard and season to taste.

Place the two heads of cauliflower upright into a deep serving dish to fit snugly together. Pour over the mustard cheese sauce and serve immediately.

Whole Cabbage on the Braai

This is a classic camping recipe, which is just as good on the coals at home as beside a smoky fire under a sky full of stars.

1 large white or green firm-headed
  cabbage, tough outer leaves
  removed
3 Tbs (90 g) butter
3 Tbs (45 ml) brown onion packet
  soup
1 cup (100 g) mature cheddar
  cheese, grated

Serves 6 – 8

Cut the cabbage in quarters without cutting straight through – cut it down to about 2 or 3 cm above the base. Gently open the cabbage up, taking care not to break it apart. Dot the butter all around the inside of the cabbage, getting in between the leaves. Then sprinkle the soup and cheese all over the inside of the cabbage. Wrap the cabbage head tightly in foil and place on the coals until soft and tender; about 35 to 40 minutes.

Cauliflower Soup with Parmesan Crisps

Don't see this recipe as an excuse to use up mature heads of cauliflower. The younger the vegetable, the more delicate the soup – and take care not to cook it for too long. The Parmesan crisps finish the dish off nicely.

2 leeks, finely sliced
1 small onion
1 clove garlic, finely chopped
1 Tbs (30 g) butter
1 Tbs (15 ml) oil
2 potatoes, peeled and diced
2 cups (500 ml) vegetable stock,
　preferably homemade
400 g cauliflower, broken into florets
1 cup (250 ml) cream
1 Tbs (15 ml) freshly squeezed
　lemon juice
1 Tbs (15 ml) Dijon mustard
1 cup (120 g) grated Parmesan, for
　the crisps
snipped chives, to serve

SERVES 4

Sauté the leeks, onion and garlic in the butter and oil until softened. Add the potato and stock, bring to the boil before reducing to a simmer. Cover and cook for about 15 minutes, until the potato has started to soften. Add the cauliflower and simmer for another 6 to 8 minutes, adding more stock if necessary. By this time the vegetables should be tender.

Remove from the heat and blend to a silky smooth consistency. Stir in the cream, lemon juice and mustard, and keep warm while you make the Parmesan crisps.

Using a greased baking tray, make 8 small piles with the grated Parmesan and spread out slightly. Place in the oven under the grill, and grill until the Parmesan melts down and turns golden. (Watch closely!) Remove from the oven and leave to cool. When the Parmesan cools it will harden, forming the 'crisps'.

Garnish the soup with snipped chives and serve with Parmesan crisps on the side.

Raw Broccoli Salad with Sweet Vinaigrette

This is a great salad to serve as an alternative to a regular Greek salad. It's a lot more interesting and nutritious (if you discount the dressing!) and it uses only three ingredients. It was first introduced to me by a dietician friend and I've been making it ever since.

THE SALAD
2 heads broccoli (use tight-head broccoli, not sprouting)
500 g baby tomatoes, halved
½ cup (75 g) pine nuts, toasted

MUSTARD DRESSING
½ cup (100 g) sugar
2 tsp (10 ml) Dijon mustard
2 tsp (10 ml) salt
⅔ cup (160 ml) white vinegar
2 cups (500 ml) canola oil

SERVES 8 – 10 AS A SIDE DISH

Break the florets off the head of broccoli and place in a salad bowl. Add the tomatoes.

To make the dressing, whisk all the ingredients together in a mixing bowl until the sugar is dissolved. (You can use olive oil if you prefer, but the fruitiness doesn't work as well with this salad.)

Pour the dressing over the broccoli and tomatoes and leave to 'marinate' for at least 20 minutes.

Scatter the pine nuts over the salad when you are ready to serve (this prevents them from getting soggy) and toss it all together.

NOTE: This recipe makes a lot of dressing (3 cups). It keeps well in the fridge, covered, for about 3 weeks.

Handmade Orecchiette with Sprouting Broccoli

Orecchiette are 'little ears' of pasta and are dead easy to make – you don't even need a pasta machine. For this dish, use the youngest tenderstem broccoli you can find. The combination of soft, steamed broccoli, soothing cream and Gorgonzola is heaven on a plate. But be warned; it's very rich.

ORECCHIETTE
1 cup (150 g) fine semolina
2 cups (240 g) plain flour
1 cup (250 ml) water

THE SAUCE
125 g sprouting broccoli tips
2 cups (500 ml) cream
180 g Gorgonzola cheese
sea salt
freshly ground black pepper

SERVES 4

For the pasta, sift the semolina and flour into a mound on a work surface dusted with flour. Make a well in the middle of the mound and pour the water into the well. (You may need more or less water depending on the quality of the flour.) Using your fingers, mix the water and flour to form dough. Knead until the dough is firm, but not sticky, about 15 minutes. Wrap in cling film and refrigerate for at least 2 hours, or overnight.

When you are ready to make the pasta, divide the dough into 8 portions. Hand-roll each portion, one at a time, into a 5 mm-thick rope, then cut 5 mm pieces from the rope. Turn cut-side up and, using your index finger or thumb, press and twist, denting the centre and forming an 'ear'. Cook in a large pot of boiling salted water for 2 minutes, or until the orecchiette begin to float. Drain.

While the pasta is boiling, steam the broccoli until softened. In a deep-sided saucepan, add the cream and crumbled cheese and bring to a simmer while stirring. Add the broccoli to the sauce and season. Add the pasta to the sauce, toss, and serve immediately.

Spinach, Sweet Pepper and Feta Phyllo Tart

This is really like a quiche, but in a phyllo 'casing'. The edges of phyllo, when left uncut and folded upwards before baking, make for a visually appetising dish that looks as good as it tastes.

1 yellow pepper, deseeded and sliced
1 red pepper, deseeded and sliced
1 large bunch spinach or chard,
  woody stalks removed, shredded
1 Tbs (15 ml) olive oil
1 Tbs (30 g) butter
1 onion, finely sliced
3 cloves garlic, finely sliced
220 g feta
3 eggs
2 extra egg yolks
1 cup (250 ml) cream
a pinch nutmeg
sea salt and black pepper
4 sheets phyllo pastry
melted butter for brushing

MAKES 1 LARGE TART

Drizzle the peppers with a little olive oil and roast in the oven for 20 minutes at 190 °C.

Steam the spinach until wilted. Place in a sieve over a bowl to drain any excess moisture. Set aside.

Heat the oil and butter and sauté the onion, adding the garlic after a few minutes. Sauté until the onion is translucent but not yet brown. Remove from the heat and add the spinach. Crumble in the feta and set aside.

In a mixing bowl, beat together the eggs, extra yolks and cream to make an egg 'custard'. Add the nutmeg and season. (Be careful not to add too much salt as feta can often be very salty.) Set aside.

Brush the sheets of phyllo with the melted butter and lay one on top of the other over a loose-bottomed 25 cm tart dish. Press the pastry into the edges of the dish and let the sides hang over (do not cut the edges to fit, rather fold upwards gently after adding the filling, trimming where necessary – it will look very beautiful after baking).

Place the spinach mix and roasted peppers into the pastry casing and pour over the egg custard. Bake in a preheated oven at 190 °C for 20 to 25 minutes, or until the phyllo is golden and the filling set. Leave to cool slightly before serving. (I find that this tart is best served at room temperature.)

Braised Red Cabbage with Apple and Cranberries

This is a brilliant dish to serve as a side. The cranberries add a festive element and the leftovers are just as delicious served at room temperature the following day.

1 onion, finely sliced
olive oil
2 Granny Smith apples, peeled
  and grated
1 red cabbage, shredded
½ cup (125 ml) red wine vinegar
sea salt and ground black pepper
1 cup (150 g) dried cranberries
1 Tbs (30 g) butter

SERVES 8 – 10 AS A SIDE DISH

In a heavy-bottomed casserole pot, sauté the onion in the oil until softened. Add the apple, cabbage and vinegar. Season to taste.

Cover with a lid and leave to cook over a low heat for about an hour, stirring occasionally. Add the cranberries and cook for another 15 minutes.

To serve, spoon into a serving dish and stir in the butter.

TIP: Prior to cooking, grate the apples at the last minute to prevent them from turning brown.

Asian Slaw with Toasted Cashew Nuts

You can use just about any type of cabbage in this recipe, but for obvious reasons the Chinese varieties are best. The important thing is the crunch and squeak of fresh leaves tossed in a mildly spiced Asian dressing of ginger, chillies, soy sauce and chopped coriander.

THE SLAW
1 small or ½ large red cabbage, shredded
1 small or ½ large Savoy cabbage, shredded
1 bunch bok choy or tatsoi, shredded
2 carrots, julienned
200 g mange tout, finely sliced
1 handful cashew nuts, toasted, crushed slightly
1 large handful fresh coriander

HONEY AND SOY DRESSING
3 Tbs (45 ml) soy sauce
3 Tbs (45 ml) freshly squeezed lime or lemon juice
dash Worcester sauce
1 clove garlic, finely chopped
3 cm fresh ginger, grated
1 Tbs (15 ml) honey
¾ cup (190 ml) extra virgin olive oil
½ cup fresh coriander, finely chopped
½ red chilli, deseeded, finely chopped

SERVES 8 AS A SIDE DISH

In a large bowl, toss together all the slaw ingredients, reserving a couple of sprigs of fresh coriander and a few toasted cashews for garnishing.

To make the dressing, whisk all the ingredients together, or shake vigorously in a jar. Taste and adjust flavours if necessary.

When you are ready to serve the slaw, mix the dressing in with the cabbage, tossing it together well to combine. Place on a platter and serve with a sprinkling of cashews and fresh coriander.

Super Juice of Black Kale, Green Apple and Ginger

Fresh vegetable juice has become something of a ritual in my household. This is my favourite. Although I use a juicer, a blender works just as well.

4 leaves of cavolo nero (black kale),
   red kale or curly leaf kale
5 Granny Smith apples
3 cm fresh ginger

SERVES 2 (MAKES ABOUT 500 ML)

Place all the ingredients in a blender or run through a juicer and drink immediately (or the apple begins to turn brown). It's delicious, promise!

OPPOSITE: *Black kale, also know as Cavolo Nero*

CHAPTER 3

Of Fruit & Flowers

Although tomatoes are broadly accepted as fruit, peppers, chillies and aubergines can be described as 'fruiting vegetables'. All part of the deadly nightshade family, myths in the nineteenth century persisted that they were a dangerous aphrodisiac, a lethal poison that led to incurable insanity. Tomatoes carried the worst reputation of all, but once accepted in European kitchens they changed cooking and eating habits around the world and became valued as vegetables in their own right.

What grows together goes together: glossy peppers, fiery chillies, plump tomatoes and shiny purple aubergines all ripen in summer at exactly the same time. Take a much-loved dish like ratatouille, for example, and you couldn't find a more perfect marriage of flavour and balance.

At around the same time of year, at the height of summer, there is a riot of colour in the vegetable patch – largely from flowering marigolds, pansies, hollyhocks and nasturtiums. These highly under-utilised salad ingredients add subtle warmth and vibrancy to salads and platters.

Another 'flower' in its own right is the globe artichoke, which forms part of the thistle family. Globe or French artichokes are the first to make an appearance in early spring and, if shamefully left uneaten, will develop into a fully blooming flower head to brighten the garden – at the expense of the table.

AUBERGINES

With names like Black Beauty, Early Long Purple and Violetta, the aubergine generally lives up to its titles. Native to India and Sri Lanka, the term 'eggplant' comes from the miniature Asian aubergines that are no larger than hen's eggs. Served on its own, this seductive vegetable – whether fried or roasted – does well with generous amounts of good olive oil to help the flesh soften and turn meltingly silky. Middle Eastern flavours enhance just about any dish involving aubergines – best of all is the classic baba ganoush, a smoky pile of creamy flesh mashed to a pulp with garlic, mint and tahini, for spreading thickly on bread or served with raw vegetable sticks for dipping.

CHILLIES

Green, red, yellow or orange, the colour of a chilli is no indication as to how hot it is. As a rule of thumb, the smaller the chilli, the hotter it's likely to be. And if you can't stand the heat, be sure to remove the seeds. The varieties are endless, from habanero and jalapeño to cayenne and bird's eye, and they can be dried, preserved or used fresh as a seasoning to add heat to soups, casseroles and sauces. Chop finely and stir into a salsa of fresh coriander and diced mango, add to a jar of preserved olives with a clove of garlic and a sprig of thyme, or drop into a broth of Asian noodles for a surprising pop of fire on the palate.

COURGETTE FLOWERS

Eaten by Italians for centuries, courgette flowers remain a novelty for most South Africans. The male flower can be picked and eaten, but pick its female counterpart and you forfeit the entire vegetable. Male blossoms have a straight stem and single stamen whereas the female flower has a bulge below the blossom. Stuffed with ricotta and mint, rolled in light batter and deep-fried until crisp, the flavour of this fragile flower is most certainly unparalleled – especially when served with a squeeze of lemon and the crystal crunch of good sea salt.

GLOBE ARTICHOKES

French or globe artichokes, with their spiky-edged leaves, are actually flower buds and, if uneaten and left to open, will form showy lilac thistle heads. But what a waste to see it bloom if you've ever tasted the delicate heart entombed beneath the petals and the hairy 'choke'. There are numerous ways to prepare this regal vegetable, but best of all is to boil it whole and peel off the petals, one by one, scraping off the buttery flesh with your teeth. They can also be stuffed, eaten whole when young enough or 'prepped' and braised in lemon, butter and wine.

NASTURTIUMS

The job of the nasturtium in any vegetable garden is to ward off pests and shade young seedlings with its umbrella-like leaves. But in the kitchen it's often overlooked. Bright yellow, shocking red and pale shades of ochre, the flowers are excellent in salads, lending the same pepperiness found in rocket, but with a more refined texture. And what could be more glorious or wonderfully romantic than eating a flower?

PEPPERS

The peppers we as South Africans are most familiar with are of the capsicum or bell pepper variety, which originate in Mexico. A member of the nightshade family, it is a fruit really, or a 'fruiting vegetable' if you like. Cut them in half and deseed and they beg to be stuffed. Leave them whole and the best result will be to roast until blackened and blistered, revealing silky, bright flesh beneath the slippery skin. This way, a drizzle of olive oil and a shred of basil is all that's required – add to salads with a hit of sheep's cheese, stir into steaming pasta with a grating of Parmesan, or pile onto a thick slice of crusty Italian bread.

TOMATOES

It should be an unwritten rule that tomatoes are eaten only in the summer months, when the punchy flavour is full and sweet. These are tomatoes that have been allowed to ripen in the sun – and on the vine. It's the ancient heirloom varieties that have the most to offer. Brandywine is a knobbly, black-green and crimson-flecked type with an almost spicy flavour; Black Cherry a dark little bauble packed with sweetness; and best of all is the Golden Monarch, a bright umber orb with masses of flavour that never fails to delight. Anybody can grow a tomato – all you need is a sunny spot and a pot, and you can grow any variety you choose.

Roast Tomato Soup with Aubergine Islands

I first saw a similar recipe in an American cookbook a few years ago. We served a version of that recipe at Café Roux for years. I've called the aubergine stacks 'islands', which is a fitting title when you see the end result of the dish – a lake of silky soup around an island of aubergine and mozzarella sandwiches. It looks beautiful and is a perfect starter for a dinner party. I've used fontina here, which is far superior to mozzarella in flavour, though you can use good mozzarella too – in fact, any melting cheese will do.

THE SOUP
8–10 tomatoes, halved or quartered
2 red onions, quartered
4 red peppers, deseeded, quartered
salt and black pepper
olive oil, for roasting
1 onion, finely sliced
2 cloves garlic, finely sliced
1 tsp (5 ml) sugar
1 handful fresh basil, torn
3 cups (750 ml) vegetable stock,
   preferably homemade
¼ cup (60 ml) fresh cream

THE AUBERGINE ISLANDS
2 large aubergines, sliced into
   2 cm thick discs
fresh basil pesto, for spreading
fontina cheese, sliced into thick
   rounds
6 slices ciabatta, sliced 2 cm thick

SERVES 6

Roast the tomatoes, red onions and peppers, seasoned and drizzled with olive oil, in a preheated oven at 220 °C for 20 to 25 minutes.

While the vegetables are roasting, sauté the white onion and garlic in a large pot until translucent but not yet browned. Add the roasted tomatoes, red onion and peppers to the pot with the sugar, basil and stock. (Add enough stock to just cover the vegetables – you don't want a soup that is too thin. Rather add less stock and adjust after blending.) Bring to the boil and simmer for just a few minutes to develop the flavours.

Blend in a food processor or use a hand blender, add the cream, then adjust the seasoning.

For the aubergine islands, season the aubergine slices and fry or grill until softened and cooked through.

Spread the aubergine slices with pesto and top with a slice of fontina. Repeat, making an aubergine, pesto and fontina stack. (You can prepare the stacks ahead of time up until this stage.)

When you are ready to serve, place the aubergine stacks on a baking tray and heat through in a preheated oven at 180 °C until the fontina begins to soften. Toast the ciabatta slices. Place each aubergine stack onto a slice of toasted ciabatta in a bowl and pour the soup around the aubergine island.

Blistered Baby Tomatoes with Feta, Olives and Basil

My mother-in-law, Mosa le Roux, introduced this dish to me. It's perfect as a pre-dinner snack for a crowd, part of a cocktail-party or canapé menu, or served with a braai. The idea is to place it all on a large platter with hunks of crusty ciabatta for mopping up the juices.

500 g baby tomatoes (use a variety
   of Rosa, cherry and heirlooms if
   you're lucky enough to have them)
salt and black pepper
olive oil, for roasting
6 feta rounds
½ cup (50 g) oven-dried
   (*see* page 81) or sun-dried
   tomatoes, sliced
10 – 12 black or kalamata
   olives, pitted
extra virgin olive oil, for drizzling
1 large handful of basil, leaves
   picked off stems
crusty ciabatta

Serves 8 – 10 as a snack

Place the tomatoes on a roasting tray, season and drizzle with olive oil. Roast in a preheated oven at 200 °C for about 20 minutes, or until the skins are split and starting to blacken ever so slightly. Remove from the oven and set aside, making sure not to discard the roasting juices.

Place the rounds of feta on a large platter so that they don't touch sides. Scatter the roasted and oven-dried tomatoes, and the olives over and around the feta.

Whisk together any remaining juices from the roast tomatoes with a bit of olive oil and drizzle over the top. Scatter over the basil leaves, and serve with ciabatta.

Vodka Gazpacho

This soup is like a Bloody Mary in a bowl. You can add as much or as little vodka as you like – or none at all. Serve it chilled and garnished with ice. It's a great little bowl for getting a dinner party started.

2 red peppers, roughly chopped
2 green peppers, roughly chopped
2 red chillies, deseeded, sliced
1 bunch spring onions, chopped
6 ripe, plum tomatoes
1 handful fresh basil
½ English cucumber
4 sticks celery
1 tsp (5 ml) sea salt
2 Tbs (30 ml) extra virgin olive oil
4 Tbs (60 ml) balsamic vinegar
1 Tbs (15 ml) sugar
4 cups (1 litre) tomato juice
Tabasco sauce, to taste
black pepper, to taste
vodka, to taste
ice cubes, for serving

SERVES 8

Place all the vegetables, along with the salt, oil, vinegar and sugar, into the bowl of a food processor and blitz. (I like my gazpacho fairly chunky, but you can blend it to your liking.)

Add enough tomato juice to get the right consistency, then adjust the seasoning, and once you're happy with it, add a dash of Tabasco, some black pepper and vodka to taste. Serve in soup bowls with an ice cube or two to 'garnish'.

Oven-dried Tomatoes

A great way to use up a glut of tomatoes, oven-drying gives a much fuller flavour than sun-drying tomatoes. And as with most things, it simply tastes better when made at home. Use them as you would sun-dried tomatoes — in salads, pasta or stirred into couscous and pilafs.

tomatoes
extra virgin olive oil, for preserving
garlic
thyme or rosemary sprigs

MAKE AS MUCH AS YOU LIKE

Make sure you use fully ripe, not over-ripe fruit. Halve or quarter the tomatoes, depending on size, and remove the pips and excess juice. Arrange on an oven rack, making sure that the sides of the tomatoes do not touch. The grill rack ensures that warm air is able to circulate all around the drying tomatoes.

Place in an oven preheated at 150 °C and make sure that you leave the door open – wedge a wooden spoon into the oven door to keep it ajar. (If you shut the door, the tomatoes will cook, rather than dry.)

Quarters should take about 3 hours to dry; halves about an hour more. It's a good idea to turn them half way through the drying time. They are ready when they crinkle and turn slightly leathery.

Place the tomatoes in sterilised jars with unpeeled garlic cloves and thyme or rosemary, completely cover with oil and secure the lids tightly. They will keep for up to 3 months. Refrigerate once the jar is open.

Avocado Salad with Nasturtiums and Quail Eggs

This is a beautiful-looking salad that is just as good to eat. Sherry vinegar can be found at select delis and farm stalls, and micro leaves, which pack a more concentrated flavour than their mature counterparts, can be found in the herb section at most supermarkets these days. Micro leaves of purple radish, red mustard, beetroot and Swiss chard are most common.

THE SALAD
12 quail's eggs
mixed leaves
micro leaves (optional)
2 ripe avocados, peeled and sliced
12 nasturtium flowers
2 Tbs (20 g) flaked almonds, toasted

ORANGE-SHERRY DRESSING
4 Tbs (60 ml) sherry vinegar
juice and zest of 1 orange
¾ cup (180 ml) extra virgin olive oil

SERVES 6

Boil the quail's eggs in a large pot for 2 minutes, remove and cool in a bowl of cold water. Peel and halve, then set aside.

For the dressing, whisk all the dressing ingredients together until well combined.

Dress the leaves, place on a large platter or in individual salad bowls, top with avocado slices, nasturtium flowers and quail's eggs, then sprinkle over the almonds, and serve.

Layered Mediterranean Crêpe Stack

This is a recipe from Cape cooking doyenne Judy Badenhorst, which we've been making and serving at the restaurant for some time. It does take a bit of effort as there are so many layers, but it's well worth the trouble, and perfect for feeding a crowd.

CRÊPES
1 cup (120 g) flour
2 eggs
½ cup (125 ml) water
1 tsp (5 ml) sunflower oil
¼ cup (60 ml) chopped chives
1 ½ cups (375 ml) milk

MEDITERRANEAN TAPENADE
1 cup (150 g) olives, pitted
1 cup (150 g) sun-dried tomatoes
120 g cream cheese
extra virgin olive oil, for blending

VEGETABLE LAYERS
5 large aubergines
8–10 courgettes, grated
2 Tbs (60 g) butter
½ cup (125 g) fresh basil pesto

For the crêpes, place all the ingredients in a large mixing bowl and mix well using a balloon whisk until you get a smooth, lump-free crêpe batter. Heat a bit of sunflower or vegetable oil in a crêpe pan, and spoon the batter in, one ladleful at a time, cooking the crêpes on both sides until golden. Set aside until ready to use.

For the tapenade, place all the ingredients (except the oil) in a food processor and blend until smooth. Add olive oil to soften to the desired consistency. Set aside.

Place the whole aubergines on a baking tray and roast in a preheated oven at 200 °C for 20 to 25 minutes. Once cool enough to handle, scoop out the flesh, discarding the skins, and purée with a hand blender. Season and set aside.

Sauté the grated courgette in a pan with the butter until softened, about 2 to 3 minutes. Season and set aside.

ROASTED TOMATO AND
RED PEPPER SAUCE

8 ripe tomatoes, halved or quartered
2 red onions, quartered
4 red peppers, deseeded, quartered
salt and black pepper
olive oil, for roasting
1 white onion, finely sliced
2 cloves garlic, finely sliced
2 tsp (10 ml) sugar
½ cup basil leaves, torn
1 cup (250 ml) vegetable stock,
  preferably homemade
grated Parmesan, for serving

SERVES 12

To make the sauce, roast the tomatoes, red onions and peppers, seasoned and drizzled with olive oil, in a preheated oven at 220 °C for 20 to 25 minutes.

While the vegetables are roasting, sauté the white onion and garlic in a large pot until translucent but not yet browned. Add the roasted tomatoes, red onions and peppers to the pot with the sugar, basil and stock. Bring to the boil, then remove from the heat and blend.

Adjust the consistency of the sauce by adding more stock if necessary. Season to taste and set aside, keeping warm.

To assemble the stack, use a greased, 25 cm-diameter loose-bottomed cake tin. Cut each crêpe to fit into the tin. Start with one crêpe laid in the tin. Spread the crêpe with a layer of tapenade, place another crêpe on top of this and spread with some basil pesto. Lay down another crêpe spread with a courgette layer, and then another spread with roasted aubergine purée.

Keep going, layering the crêpes and sandwiching each layer with one of the fillings until you have reached the top of the cake tin. (You can assemble the crêpe stack up until here at least one day in advance.)

To serve, place the tin in a preheated oven at 180 °C until heated through (about 20 minutes). Remove from the tin and slice into wedges. Serve with the roasted tomato and red pepper sauce and grated Parmesan.

OVERLEAF: *Layered Mediterranean crêpe stack*

Courgette Flowers Stuffed with Ricotta and Mint

The addition of egg whites to the beer batter makes for a light, crispy crust, which complements the delicate flavour of the flowers. The lemon wedges and salt are an absolute must for serving.

THE FLOWERS
12 courgette flowers, stamens
  removed
vegetable oil, for frying
salt flakes, to serve
lemon wedges, to serve

THE STUFFING
250 g ricotta
¼ cup (60 ml) finely chopped
  mint leaves
1 tsp (5 ml) lemon zest
sea salt
freshly ground black pepper

THE BATTER
1¼ cups (150 g) plain flour
1 tsp (5 ml) salt
1½ cups (375 ml) chilled
  lager-style beer
3 egg whites, stiffly beaten

MAKES 12 FRIED BLOSSOMS

To make the filling, combine all the stuffing ingredients in a bowl. Using a spoon, carefully fill each blossom with about 1 tablespoon of the ricotta mixture. Twist the tips of the petals to close. Set aside while you make the batter.

To make the batter, combine the flour and salt in a large bowl, then whisk in the beer to form a smooth batter (take care not to over-whisk as the batter will deflate). Fold in the beaten egg whites carefully.

To fry the courgette flowers, heat about 5 cm of oil in a deep-sided saucepan. One by one, dredge the courgette flowers in the batter, shaking off any excess, and lay in the oil, without overcrowding the pan. Fry, turning once, until golden and crispy.

Drain on paper towels and serve immediately with salt flakes and lemon wedges.

Warm Spaghetti Salad with Red Pesto and Tomatoes

This is the ideal last-minute meal for supper when all you have is a well-stocked pantry and a couple of fresh tomatoes, rocket from the garden and a bit of cheese. I like to use wild rocket, purely because it looks prettier. You can substitute the feta with goat's chevin or Parmesan cheese. The idea is to stir in all the cold, fresh ingredients as soon as you drain the pasta, so the end result will be warm rather than hot – the perfect ending to a hot summer's day.

500 g spaghetti
250 g baby tomatoes (cherry
  or Rosa)
350 g large tomatoes (plum or
  Roma), halved
4 Tbs (60 g) sun-dried tomato pesto
  (shop-bought is fine, but try to get
  the fresh version)
1 handful of rocket
black or kalamata olives, pitted
1 round feta
extra virgin olive oil, for drizzling
basil leaves, to garnish

SERVES 4

Cook the spaghetti in a large pot of boiling, salted water.

While the spaghetti is cooking, pan-roast a handful of the baby tomatoes in a little olive oil until the skins split. Stir them into the remaining fresh tomatoes and set aside. Combining fresh and roasted tomatoes adds flavour and contrasting textures to this dish.

When the pasta is cooked, drain and reserve half a cup of the cooking water. In the same pot, immediately stir in the pesto and toss through the rocket leaves, tomatoes and olives. Working quickly in the still-hot cooking pot will ensure a warm dish.

If it seems a bit dry, loosen it up with a dash of the reserved cooking liquid. Divide into serving bowls, crumble over the feta and drizzle with olive oil. Serve immediately.

Tomato Party Tart

This tart is a celebration of tomatoes — fresh and oven-dried tomatoes, as well as sun-dried tomato pesto spread thickly over the puff pastry. You can use any size or shape of tomato, but be sure to halve or quarter large ones. This is the sort of thing that can be prepared in advance and banged in the oven just before serving. The variety in colour and size makes for a very festive looking tart.

1 roll all-butter puff pastry
½ cup (125 g) sun-dried tomato
  pesto
500 g tomatoes, all shapes and sizes
1 handful sun-dried or oven-dried
  tomatoes (*see* page 81)
1 handful fresh thyme
sea salt
freshly ground black pepper
melted butter, for brushing

MAKES 1 LARGE TART

Make sure that the puff pastry is thawed, but still chilled. It won't puff up nearly as well if it's not well chilled. Brush the pastry all over with pesto, leaving a 1 cm frame around the edge.

Scatter the tomatoes over the pesto, making sure to halve or quarter the larger ones. Scatter over the oven-dried tomatoes and thyme leaves, and season well. Brush the edges of the pastry with the melted butter.

Place in a preheated oven at 200 °C for 25 to 30 minutes, or until the pastry edges are golden and risen and the tomatoes beginning to blister. Serve hot or at room temperature.

Two Pâtés

It's no picnic without a pâté. Here are two that celebrate the vegetables from which they are made.

ARTICHOKE & LEMON PÂTÉ
2 cloves garlic, unpeeled
6–8 cooked artichoke hearts, or
    2 cans (800 g) tinned, drained
    hearts
juice and zest of 1 lemon
4 heaped Tbs cream cheese
½ cup (60 g) freshly grated
    Parmesan
extra virgin olive oil
warm water, to thin

If you use fresh artichoke hearts in this recipe, you will be rewarded with sublime flavour. Of course you can use canned artichoke hearts, and it will still be delicious. The cream cheese gives it a lovely smooth texture and the Parmesan takes it to new heights.

Place the garlic, artichoke hearts, lemon juice and zest into the bowl of a food processor or blender. Blend until smooth, then add the cream cheese and Parmesan, and blend again. Add a generous drizzle of olive oil to taste. Thin with warm water if necessary. Serve with crusty bread or crackers.

ROASTED AUBERGINE PÂTÉ
4 aubergines
2 cloves garlic
juice of 2 lemons
4 Tbs (60 ml) tahini
1 handful Italian parsley
1 handful mint
1 Tbs (15 ml) cumin
a pinch white pepper
200 g plain yoghurt
4 Tbs (40 g) toasted pine nuts

This is my take on the North African *baba ganoush*. Don't hold back on the mint and parsley – not only do they enhance the flavour, but the herbs give this pâté a lovely green tinge.

Rub the aubergines with olive oil and bake in a preheated oven at 200 °C until the skins are blistered and blackened. Remove from the oven, place in a bowl and cover with cling film. Set aside.

When cool, peel the skin off and place the flesh in a colander and leave to drain for about 10 minutes. Place in a food processor with the rest of the ingredients (except for the yoghurt and pine nuts) and blend until smooth.

Stir in the yoghurt and season to taste. Sprinkle with toasted pine nuts and serve.

EACH RECIPE
MAKES 2 CUPS

Marinated Aubergine

This is a very easy method of making pickles that can be eaten with cheese or used in salads and on sandwiches. The marinade literally pickles the aubergine when left overnight.

4 aubergines sliced into paper-thin
  rounds, or diced

MARINADE
2 cups (500 ml) white wine vinegar
1 cup (250 ml) tepid water
2 cups (500 ml) olive oil
2 Tbs (30 ml) coriander seeds
4 cloves garlic, whole
2 chillies, whole
2 Tbs (30 ml) dried mixed herbs

MAKES 2 JARS

Mix all the marinade ingredients together. Place the aubergine into the marinade, cover and refrigerate overnight. The aubergine will soften beautifully and absorb all the flavours of the marinade. The pickle will keep for up to 2 weeks in the fridge.

If you would like to preserve them for longer, place the pickled aubergines in sterilised jars, completely cover with the marinade and secure the lids tightly. They will keep for up to 3 months. Refrigerate once the jar is open.

Baked Aubergine with Tomatoes, Thyme and Cream

This is a take on a wildly popular recipe from my first book, Prickly Pears & Pomegranates. *The addition of aubergine makes it more substantial. I prefer to use whole, baby aubergines, but you can also use cubed aubergine — only, it won't look as pretty.*

8 baby aubergines or 2 large
  aubergines, cubed
olive oil, for frying
a selection of baby tomatoes
sun-dried or oven-dried tomatoes
  (*see* page 81)
fresh thyme leaves
salt and black pepper
1 ½ cups (375 ml) cream
1 cup (120 g) grated Parmesan

SERVES 4 AS A MAIN,
OR 6 AS A SIDE DISH

If using baby aubergines, halve, drizzle with olive oil and place on a baking tray (cut-side facing down) in a preheated oven at 200 °C for 15 minutes.

If using large aubergines, sprinkle the cubes with salt to draw out excess moisture. This will reduce the amount of oil used when frying and remove any bitterness. Leave for about 30 minutes, then rinse under cold, running water. Pat dry with paper towels. In a saucepan, heat the olive oil and then fry the aubergine cubes, turning, until golden and cooked; about 15 minutes. Drain on paper towels.

In a baking dish, roughly layer the fresh and dried tomatoes and aubergine interspersed with thyme leaves and a sprinkling of Parmesan. Season (keeping in mind the salted aubergine), and pour over the cream.

Grate a generous amount of Parmesan over the top and place in a preheated oven at 180 °C for 35 to 40 minutes, or until golden and bubbling.

Braised Globe Artichokes with Crushed Broad Beans

Globe artichokes and broad beans are in season at exactly the same time of year, which makes them perfect partners. Make the most of this dish, as the time is short-lived.

4–6 globe or French artichokes
2 cups broad beans
2 Tbs (60 g) butter
juice of 1 lemon
sea salt
ground black pepper

SERVES 4 AS A SIDE DISH

To prepare the artichokes, remove the tough outer leaves. Using a pair of kitchen scissors, trim off all the sharp, thorny tips and cut about a centimetre off the top. Quarter and, using a teaspoon, scoop out the hairy choke at the heart of the artichoke. Place in boiling, salted water and cook until tender. Set aside.

Place the broad beans in a pot of boiling water and blanch for about 2 minutes. Strain and slip off the outer membrane (unless using very young broad beans, in which case you can use them just as they are after blanching). Place the broad beans in a bowl and, using a potato masher or the back of a spoon, press down ever so slightly, squashing and crushing them a little.

Heat a saucepan and melt the butter. Add the lemon juice, artichokes and crushed broad beans. Sauté until heated through and coated in the lemon and butter. Season liberally with salt and pepper. Serve immediately.

Ultimate Grilled Vegetable Sandwich

This is a sandwich we served at Café Roux for years. When I tried to take it off the menu there was an outcry from the locals who would come especially for it. It's a marriage of good ingredients that harmonise beautifully. (Great for using up left-over roast vegetables from Sunday lunch.)

**mixed peppers, deseeded, cut into
   broad pieces**
aubergine, sliced into 1 cm rounds
courgettes, sliced lengthwise
salt and black pepper
olive oil, for grilling
**beetroot, roasted, optional
   (*see* page 26)**
rocket
ciabatta, sliced, buttered
buffalo mozzarella, sliced
basil pesto, to serve

Make as many as you like

Place all the vegetables (except the beetroot) on an oven tray, season, drizzle with olive oil and place under the grill. Leave the oven door ajar by wedging in a wooden spoon. (This helps get rid of the steam, so your vegetables will be 'drier' than if you grilled them with the door closed.)

Watch them closely and turn when they begin to colour. Remove from the oven when slightly golden and cooked through; after about 20 minutes.

Place the mozzarella on the ciabatta and place under the grill until the cheese turns golden. Top with the grilled vegetables and roasted beetroot (if using), and place the rocket on top. Serve with some basil pesto on the side.

Hollyhock Salad with Artichokes and Toasted Pine Nuts

Hollyhock flowers are extremely pretty but need a nutty element for balance. Here I've used toasted pine nuts. It's a salad you'll be proud to place on any table.

MUSTARD DRESSING
½ cup (100 g) sugar
2 tsp (10 ml) Dijon mustard
2 tsp (10 m) salt
⅔ cup (160 ml) white vinegar
2 cups (500 ml) canola oil

CROUTONS
4 slices day-old ciabatta
olive oil

HOLLYHOCK SALAD
½ cup (75 g) pine nuts
6–8 artichokes
mixed leaves
1 wedge Parmesan, for shaving
8 hollyhock flowers

SERVES 4

To make the dressing, whisk all the ingredients together in a mixing bowl until the sugar is dissolved. (You can use olive oil if you prefer, but the fruitiness doesn't work as well with this salad.) Set aside. This recipe makes about 3 cups of dressing. Remaining dressing can be stored, covered, in the fridge for up to 3 weeks.

To make the croutons, tear up the ciabatta into rough chunks. Scatter onto a baking tray and drizzle liberally with olive oil. Place in a preheated oven at 200 °C until golden and crispy.

Scatter the pine nuts evenly onto a separate baking tray and toast them at the same time as the croutons. Keep a close watch on them so that they don't burn. Set aside.

To prepare the artichokes, remove the tough outer leaves. Using a pair of kitchen scissors, trim off all the sharp, thorny tips and cut about a centimetre off the top. Quarter and, using a teaspoon, scoop out the hairy choke at the heart of the artichoke. Place in boiling, salted water and cook until tender. Set aside.

To serve, divide the leaves among four salad plates. Place the artichoke quarters on the leaves and scatter the croutons over the top. Using a potato peeler, shave the Parmesan evenly over each salad and add the toasted pine nuts and hollyhocks. Dress just before serving.

Chapter 4

Climbers & Sprawlers

One of my earliest memories is of rows and rows of enormous white pumpkins, stored by the hundred, on just about every flat roof on the farm. The Karoo is known for having fields full of sprawling pumpkins that need to be harvested by the end of summer, to save them from impending frost, before being left to dry in the crisp winter sun on the roofs of outbuildings. We would eat pumpkin all winter, but never tired of it in all its guises. We had pumpkin fritters dusted liberally with cinnamon sugar; golden, honey-baked wedges with a whisper of orange zest; sticky, roasted cubes of sweetness; hearty soups and wholesome casseroles. It was pumpkin heaven.

Squash is another rambler that enjoys some space in the garden. Summer squashes are picked when they are immature; the whole vegetable – skin and seed – is edible, whereas winter squash varieties are picked when they are fully grown and have tough, inedible skins with hard seeds. Some of my favourites are the golden hubbard squash with its delicate sweetness, black-and-green ribbed acorn squash and, of course, the squash *du jour* – butternut.

Climbing beans and peas are another sight to behold in the vegetable patch – especially the garden pea, with its delicate tendrils twisting up wigwams and trellises, its bone-white flowers glistening in the sunshine. Beans are happy to make their way up wire frames or sticks of cane, secured with string and tightly bound against the wind. Climbing beans include flat, slightly coarse runner beans, and the more refined French bean. Whatever the variety, their uses in the kitchen are countless. I like beans best when steamed and sautéed in a generous knob of butter, or blanched and added to salads – a bowlful of glorious green goodness with a crisp crunch-lending texture.

BEANS

In the garden, climbing French and runner beans curl their way up frames, looping around supports, while smaller bush beans don't get much bigger than knee-high. Purple King is a striking purple-blue bush bean that sadly turns green when cooked, but thankfully the yellow-podded Roquefort and Yellow Dwarf retain their golden hue after cooking. Blanched and tossed in butter the combination makes for a beautiful side dish. Painted Lady, an ancient runner introduced in the seventeenth century, is an unusual violent pink when you split open the green pod (*see* A Note on Heirlooms on page 11). French beans, more refined than runner beans, are rounder and shorter than the heavier runner; both are also known as string beans, a name derived from the coarse 'string' appearing along the seams of the pod. (However, the development of stringless varieties has made the term almost obsolete.)

BROAD BEANS

Broad beans are one of those vegetables that come around only once a year for a very short period of time. It's the kind of thing I can happily eat every day for six weeks, have my fill and then wait until the next season, by which time I'm craving them beyond measure all over again. There's such beauty in opening a pod of broad beans – press down on the curved edge near one end to pop the pod open revealing a velvet case of perfectly formed beans, each encased in its very own protective skin. There are two ways to peel this membrane off each bean: blanch in boiling water and simply slip off the skin; or use a thumbnail to split the fresh, opaque layer at the bean's indented eye, and pull carefully away.

PEAS

Pop open a pod of peas in early summer and the fresh sweetness that fills the mouth is unparalleled. Tiny, young peas – the French call them *petit pois* – are tender and sweet; they appear in markets in spring and early summer and require only the briefest of boiling. As summer advances they get bigger, the natural sugar gradually turns to starch and the texture becomes mealy; medium-sized peas need more time in the pot and large ones are best reserved for soups and purées. *Mange tout* (meaning 'eat it all') is a short, flat pod with barely developed seeds, which is eaten in its entirety. And never, ever frown upon a frozen pea. It has to be the most consistent of all vegetables.

PUMPKINS

Winter pumpkins are the tough-skinned, golden-fleshed cousins of the more delicate pale green and yellow summer squash. Once you've hacked through the tough exterior, the sweet flesh within is the greatest reward. Most pumpkins hold a high water content and need to be cooked with little or no water in the pot to avoid a sloppy end result. The exotic-looking Turks Turban, shaped like Aladdin's hat, is a favourite heirloom variety for its manageable size and tasty flesh. Our very own South African *Wit boerpampoen* has also recently been labelled an heirloom, as it was in danger of losing its true essence due to hybridisation (*see* A Note on Heirlooms on page 11).

SQUASH

Squash growing in the garden is a beautiful thing to behold. Some climb up trellises and wigwams, others sprawl amongst nasturtiums; green, yellow and gold-flecked orbs glowing in the sun. They bring colour and brightness into the kitchen too – chunks of golden butternut against the red sauce of tomatoes; bright yellow patty pans in a dish of green courgettes. Stuffed with rice, thyme and toasted pine nuts, acorn squash is a great one to bake (perhaps with a handful of Parmesan thrown in for good measure). And then there's the baby gem squash – no bigger than a golf ball – which is near perfect steamed and served with dripping butter and a rasping of nutmeg. The options with squash are endless.

Crispy Butternut Salad

For the crunchiest butternut crisps it's best to deep-fry the shavings. If you'd prefer a healthier option, you can bake them in a preheated oven at 200 °C, but they will require regular turning and often don't crisp up as evenly. It's a good idea to dress just the salad leaves before arranging the salad to prevent the crisps from becoming soggy.

SALAD

1 medium butternut, peeled
300 g mixed leaves
½ cup (50 g) oven-dried
  (*see* page 81) or sun-dried
  tomatoes, sliced
1 log chevin goat's cheese
1 wedge Gruyere cheese, for shaving
1 cup (150 g) mix of sunflower and
  pumpkin seeds, toasted

HONEY AND BALSAMIC DRESSING

3 Tbs (45 ml) balsamic vinegar
3 Tbs (45 ml) freshly squeezed
  lemon juice
1 clove garlic, finely chopped
3 cm fresh ginger, grated
1 Tbs (15 ml) raw honey
¾ cup (190 ml) extra virgin olive oil

SERVES 6

Use a potato peeler to peel long, thin shavings of butternut flesh. Have a pot of hot oil at the ready and deep-fry the shavings in batches. Leave to drain on kitchen paper.

To make the dressing, place all the ingredients, except the olive oil, in a blender or food processor and blend to combine. Pour into a bowl and whisk in the oil.

On a large platter (I like to use a big, flat platter), or in individual salad bowls, scatter a generous quantity of mixed leaves. Dress the leaves and toss well. Top with butternut shavings, sun-dried tomatoes and rounds of goat's cheese.

Using the potato peeler, shave strips of Gruyere and arrange around the platter. Scatter over the toasted seeds and serve.

Green Pea and Broad Bean Hummus

A fresh and tasty alternative to chickpea hummus, broad beans and peas have the added advantage of lending that vibrant colour so lacking in chickpeas. I like this hummus best served with crisp chicory leaves for dipping, but it's just as good with crusty bread or crackers.

250 g broad beans, podded
250 g fresh or frozen peas
2 cloves garlic, peeled and crushed
juice of 1 lemon
6 Tbs (90 ml) extra virgin olive oil
sea salt and ground black pepper
1 handful mint, roughly chopped

MAKES 2 CUPS

Blanch the broad beans in boiling water for about 2 minutes. Once they have cooled enough to handle, slip off the outer membranes. (They should come off easily.)

If using fresh peas, add them to boiling water and cook for about 10 minutes until softened. If using frozen, boil for about 2 minutes.

Place all the ingredients in a food processor and blend until smooth. Season to taste.

Bean Salad with Feta, Red Onion and Mint

Bean salads can be incredibly versatile – this is my version using both fresh and canned beans, mint and red onion. It's packed with flavour and makes for perfect picnic food.

BEAN SALAD
400 g fresh broad beans, podded
6–8 runner beans, cut into 2 cm
  slices on the diagonal
1 can cannellini beans, drained and
  rinsed
1 can kidney beans, drained and
  rinsed
2 celery stalks, finely sliced
½ red onion, finely chopped
½ cup (125 ml) fresh flat leaf parsley,
  finely chopped
½ cup (125 ml) fresh mint, finely
  sliced
1 red pepper, finely sliced
lemon juice, to taste
feta, to serve

DRESSING
½ cup (125 ml) apple cider vinegar
1 Tbs (15 ml) sugar
½ cup (125 ml) olive oil
½ cup (125 ml) sunflower oil
sea salt and cracked black pepper,
  to taste

SERVES 6–8

Blanch the broad beans in boiling, salted water for about 2 minutes. Remove the beans from the pot, cool under cold running water and slip off the outer membrane. Return the broad beans to the pot of boiling water, together with the runner bean slices and cook for a further 2 minutes. Drain and set aside.

In a large bowl, mix the canned beans, celery, onion, parsley, mint and red pepper.

To make the dressing, whisk together all the dressing ingredients, add to the beans and toss to coat. Chill in the refrigerator to allow the beans to soak up the dressing.

To serve, add a squeeze of lemon and some chunks of feta.

Peas and Broad Beans with Crème Fraîche and Mint

Peas and broad beans make an appearance in the garden at the same time of year, which is a general indication that they will go together on the plate. Both are delicious with mint, and crème fraîche rounds the dish off nicely.

1 ½ cups (225 g) fresh podded peas,
   or frozen peas
1 ½ cups (225 g) podded broad
   beans
4 Tbs (60 ml) crème fraîche
1 handful fresh mint, finely chopped

SERVES 4 AS A SIDE DISH

Boil the peas in a pot of boiling water for about 10 minutes if using fresh, or 2 minutes if using frozen.

In a separate pot, blanch the broad beans until the outer membrane slips off easily. Cool under cold running water and slip the shells off. Add to the pot with the peas for the last 2 minutes of cooking time.

Strain off the water, return to the pot, and add the crème fraîche until heated through. Stir in the mint and serve.

Pea Risotto with Lemon and Mint

This is a dish I make very often at home. Fresh peas are great, but frozen peas work just as well. I always have frozen peas in my freezer and risotto rice in the pantry. Children love it too — but go easy on the mint.

4 cups (1 litre) vegetable stock,
   preferably homemade
1 onion, finely chopped
2 Tbs (30 ml) olive oil
350 g Arborio rice
½ wine glass of dry white wine
zest and juice of 1 lemon
2 cups (300 g) fresh or frozen peas
1 knob butter
1 handful mint, finely chopped
1 very large handful good-quality
   Parmesan
salt and black pepper

SERVES 6

Make sure you have a pot of stock on a low heat on the stove before you start the risotto, as you want to add hot stock to the rice to prevent it from losing heat.

In a heavy-bottomed pot, sauté the onion in the oil until softened, but not golden. Add the rice and sauté, stirring constantly, until the edges of the grains of rice become slightly translucent. Add the wine and cook until it is absorbed by the rice.

Now start adding the stock, one ladle at a time, only adding the next ladle once the previous one has been completely absorbed by the rice. The whole process should take about 20 minutes, by which time the rice should have softened nicely.

You can now add the lemon zest and peas. Continue cooking and stirring until the peas are cooked.

Once the rice is completely cooked, remove from the heat, and add the butter, lemon juice, mint and Parmesan. Give it a good stir and set aside, covered, for 2 minutes to allow the flavours to develop.

Serve immediately as risotto does not like to be reheated. Spoon onto six individual plates or bowls and serve with a wedge of Parmesan for grating extra cheese over the top.

Garden Pea and Rocket Pesto Soup

There is absolutely nothing wrong with using frozen peas for this recipe, yet the difference in flavour if using freshly podded peas is astounding. Basil pesto can be used as a substitute for rocket pesto, but you'll miss the pepperiness it imparts.

ROCKET PESTO
1 small clove garlic
2 handfuls rocket
¾ cup (120 g) pine nuts, toasted
½ cup (60 g) grated Parmesan
extra virgin olive oil, to taste
salt and pepper
lemon juice, to taste

GARDEN PEA SOUP
1 onion, sliced
2 Tbs olive oil
3 cups (750 ml) vegetable stock,
  preferably homemade
375 g fresh (or frozen) peas
salt and pepper
2 Tbs sour cream (optional)

SERVES 4

Make the rocket pesto first. You can use a food processor or pestle and mortar; I prefer using a pestle and mortar as it gives more control over consistency and texture.

Pound the garlic in a pestle and mortar. Add the rocket and keep pounding until the rocket breaks down. Add the pine nuts and pound to a rough, chunky paste. Tumble into a bowl and stir in the Parmesan. Stir in enough olive oil to reach the preferred consistency. Season and add a squeeze of lemon juice to taste.

For the soup, sauté the onion in the oil until softened. Add the stock and bring to the boil, then add the peas. If using fresh peas, simmer for 8 to 10 minutes. If using frozen, simmer for 2 minutes. Pour the peas and stock into a food processor or blender and add 5 tablespoons of rocket pesto. Blend until smooth. Season to taste.

To serve, heat the soup and add the sour cream (if using). Serve with crusty bread.

Pumpkin Laksa

Laksa is a spicy noodle soup originating in Malaysia and Indonesia. It has all the punchy flavours you'd expect from these two countries – the fiery hit of ginger and chillies, aromatic scent of lemon grass, the tang of limes and saltiness of fish sauce. You can use most types of pumpkin or squash you have at hand.

2 – 3 lime leaves

3 chillies, deseeded and chopped

2 lemon grass stalks, roughly chopped

4 shallots or one small red onion, peeled and chopped

2 cloves garlic, peeled and chopped

4 cm fresh ginger

1 tsp (5 ml) turmeric

1 tsp (5 ml) Chinese five-spice powder

700 g pumpkin, butternut or Hubbard squash, peeled and chopped into 5 cm chunks

2 cups (500 ml) vegetable stock, preferably homemade

2 x 400 ml cans coconut milk

juice of 2 limes

1 Tbs (15 ml) fish sauce

300 g rice noodles

1 handful bean sprouts

1 handful fresh mint, torn

1 handful fresh basil, torn

SERVES 6

Using a food processor, or pestle and mortar, blend or pound together the lime leaves, chillies, lemon grass, shallots, garlic, ginger, turmeric and five-spice to form a chunky paste.

Add the paste to a heavy-bottomed pot and cook, stirring, for about 2 minutes. Add the pumpkin and stock, bring to the boil, then simmer, uncovered, until the pumpkin is soft; about 20 minutes.

Add the coconut milk, lime juice and fish sauce. In the meantime, cook the noodles as per the instructions on the packet.

To serve, divide the noodles amongst six serving bowls, ladle over the soup and garnish generously with bean sprouts, mint and basil.

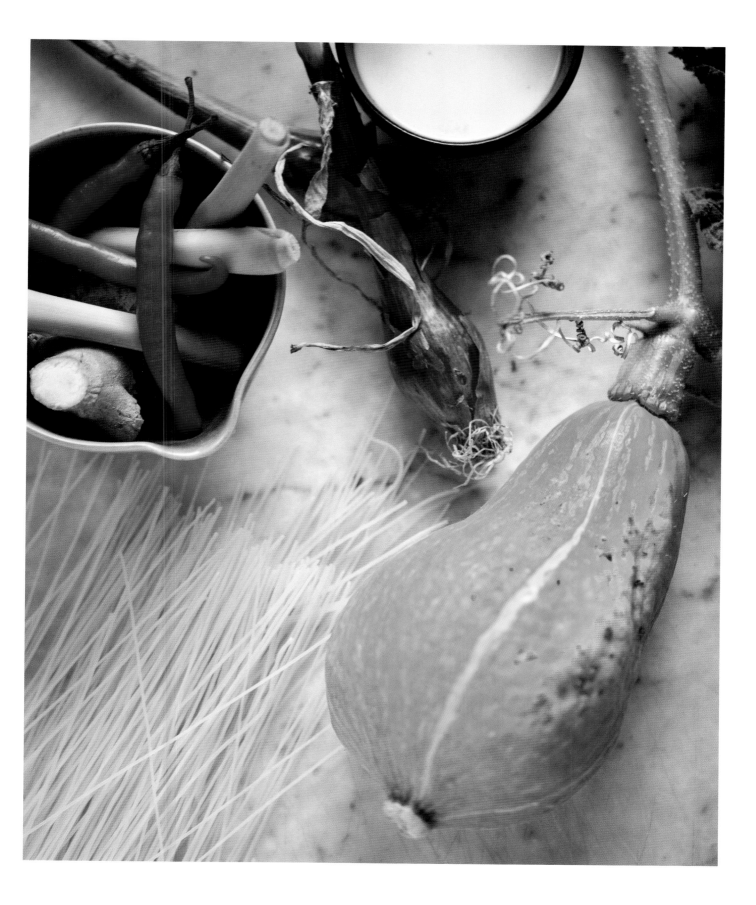

Pumpkin and Squash Gratin

The beauty of this recipe is that you can use any pumpkin or squash you please. I like a combination of Hubbard squash, butternut and Turks Turban pumpkin.

1 onion, sliced
2 Tbs (60 g) butter
1 butternut or medium hubbard
   squash, peeled and sliced evenly
300 g pumpkin, peeled and sliced
   evenly
small bunch fresh thyme
sea salt and ground black pepper
2 cups (500 ml) cream
1 large handful grated Parmesan

SERVES 6−8 AS A SIDE DISH

Sauté the onion slices in the butter over a low heat until just beginning to turn golden. Set aside.

In a roasting dish, layer the butternut and pumpkin slices, sautéed onion and herbs, seasoning between each layer. Pour over the cream and bake in a preheated oven at 220 °C for 20 minutes.

Add the Parmesan and bake for another 20 minutes or until the pumpkin is soft and golden.

Gnocchi with Butternut and Gorgonzola Cream

Gnocchi may sound – and look – intimidating to make, but follow a few essential rules and you'll be making it blindfolded in no time. It really is worth the effort as the potato balls will be light and melt-in-the-mouth compared with the doughy bought version. First things first: make sure you have a potato ricer. Be warned: this is a rich dish and I find it's best served as a starter.

THE GNOCCHI

6 large floury potatoes
1 egg
1 cup (120 g) all-purpose flour
1 tsp (5 ml) salt

RULE 1: The type of potato you use is very important. It absolutely has to be a floury or starchy potato and not a waxy variety. (Waxy potatoes hold their shape and tend to make lumps.) Place the potatoes on a baking tray and bake in the oven at 190 °C for 45 to 50 minutes, by which time the skins will be crispy and the inside fluffy and soft.

RULE 2: Baking the potatoes keeps them dry; boiling would result in 'wet' potato flesh, resulting in claggy balls of gnocchi.

RULE 3: Work while your potatoes are still hot! This can be tricky, so you may have to wear oven gloves to scoop out the flesh. Cut each potato in half, scoop out the flesh and push through a potato ricer into a large mixing bowl.

Add the egg, flour and salt to the potatoes in the mixing bowl and knead quickly. If the dough is very sticky, you can add a bit more flour, but be careful not to add too much flour or your dumplings will be heavy. When you hold the dough in your hands it should be very soft to the touch; it should be moist and 'billowy', but not sticky.

Dust some flour over your work surface. Break off balls of dough, slightly larger than a golf ball, and roll gently into snake-shaped logs, about the thickness of a thumb. Dust with a bit more flour. Using a sharp knife, cut the 'log' into 2 cm lengths.

(Gnocchi freezes beautifully, so if you aren't going to be cooking it immediately, you're better off freezing the dumplings at this stage.)

BUTTERNUT AND
GORGONZOLA CREAM
½ small butternut squash
2 cups (500 ml) cream
180 g Gorgonzola
sea salt
freshly ground black pepper

SERVES 6 AS A STARTER

To cook, drop the dumplings into boiling, salted water. The beauty about cooking gnocchi, is that they sink to the bottom of the pot when you drop them into boiling water and start to float once they are cooked. Remove the floating gnocchi from the pot as they rise to the surface, using a slotted spoon. Set aside and keep warm while you make the sauce.

To make the sauce, steam or boil the squash until very soft. Purée in a food processor, or use a hand blender. Place a deep-sided saucepan or pot on the stove and pour in the cream. Break the gorgonzola into pieces and drop into the cream, slowly melting the cheese over a low heat, until the cream has thickened and reduced slightly and all the cheese has melted. Add the puréed squash and stir using a whisk until smooth and creamy. If the sauce is too thick, thin with a little vegetable stock. Season to taste.

Turn off the heat and add the cooked gnocchi to the sauce, making sure the dumplings are evenly coated in sauce. Serve immediately.

Buttered Baby Gems with Nutmeg

There really is nothing on earth like baby gem squash, steamed and halved, with a knob of melting butter and a whisper of nutmeg.

12 baby gem squash
butter, to serve
salt, to taste
nutmeg, to taste

SERVES 6

Place the baby gems in a steamer (they hold their shape better than if you were to boil them) and steam for 15 to 20 minutes, or until soft.

I like to cut them in half so that the butter can melt into them, but you could serve them whole too. Season with salt and nutmeg, and serve.

CHAPTER 5

Wild Things

My great-aunt, and legendary author, Eve Palmer instilled in me a fascination with weeds and *veldkos* or 'pot weeds' (as she liked to refer to them) – most of which can be found in urban gardens. Things like pigweed, blackjacks, chickweed, dandelion and nettles have been eaten in Africa for centuries – more out of necessity than for pleasure, however. Many of the more popular weeds, such as sorrel, purslane and dandelion leaves are now grown commercially. But if you're picking your own, it's best to pick in spring, before the plant flowers and while the leaves are still young.

Of all the ingredients that can be foraged from the wild it is surely the elusive porcini mushroom that is most coveted. Porcini and ceps are technically the same thing, the former being the Italian term and the latter, French. Whatever the name, mushroom hunters become almost obsessive about this prized ingredient with the distinctive sponge formation under its giant cap. In South Africa we're lucky to have porcini almost all year round. In the Western Cape they grow in autumn and into winter, and in the summer rainfall areas further up north porcini are available in summer. I like them best sautéed with garlic and shallots, a shot of brandy and a spoon of mascarpone in the pan, then served on toasted sourdough. The humble and underrated pine ring mushroom is unfortunately overshadowed by the glamour of the porcini. Pine rings lend a beautiful orange

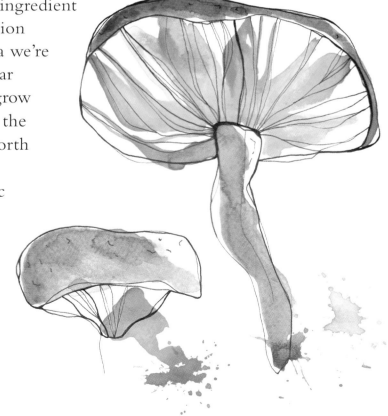

glow to dishes and have a delicate, mild – though very wild – flavour. Pine rings are good with just about any recipe that involves eggs and cream.

As far as sea vegetables go, samphire is now commercially available. Known as poor-man's asparagus, it is both sweet and salty, woody and delicate. All that's required is a gentle steam, a knob of butter and a squeeze of lemon.

With foraging rising in popularity it's important to go carefully. There are unwritten rules and an element of etiquette required when it comes to foraging: many wild plants are protected, in which case they should be left alone; take care not to damage the plant – when picked correctly it will regenerate; do not collect mushrooms without an experienced guide; and never, ever forage on private land without permission.

NETTLES

Even though they invade flowerbeds and ditches with wild abandon, stinging nettles have a long history as edible weeds. The 'sting' is broken down in cooking, yet it's best to eat only the young, soft-textured leaves, which are high in iron and hold a reputation for having great blood-purifying properties. Most people are familiar with nettle soup – a dense and delicious dark green – but nettles are good in risottos, egg dishes and casseroles too. But be warned: it's best to wear decent gloves when handling them.

PINE RING MUSHROOMS
(Lactarius deliciosus)

Pine rings are best identified by a prominent neon orange ring on the inside of the stalk when sliced, and the deep, almost fluorescent-orange colour on the underside of the cap. Be warned that the similarly coloured Copper Trumpet is deadly poisonous. Come autumn and a few days of rain followed by two days of glorious sunshine make for the best foraging conditions. They grow in the deep shade of pine forests, usually covered by a blanket of pine needles. Look out for little heaps of needles, brush them aside and there will no doubt be a mushroom or two hidden underneath. Pine rings and eggs are a great combination – serve them sautéed in butter and thyme atop scrambled eggs or baked in a frittata with chilli and chard.

PORCINI MUSHROOMS
(Boletus edulis)

These enormous mushrooms do not have gills underneath the cap, but a uniform, spongy and porous texture. When picked correctly, porcini appear in the exact same location year after year, hence the secretive nature of the experienced mushroom hunter. Porcini lend themselves to rich, comforting and creamy dishes: a dark risotto of thyme and porcini; steaming bowls of wild mushroom soup with a hit of lemon zest and crème fraîche; gnocchi with a buttery reduction of wine and ceps. And always a great big handful of good Parmesan. Whatever you do with them, make sure you get these hidden gems from a trusted source and never, ever forage for mushrooms without an experienced guide.

PURSLANE

Purslane, also commonly known as portulaca, is a succulent annual that forms a mat of reddish green shiny stems and tiny yellow flowers. Thought to have been planted by early sailors along the coastline, purslane spread rapidly inland with the movement of cattle. It can be eaten cooked or raw. I like it best in salads. Succulent and bouncy, the clover-like leaves add a clean, fresh bite to salads and are high on many chefs' most-wanted list of leaves. One of my favourite methods of eating purslane is scattered over marinated cucumber strips with sliced red chillies and topped with homemade labneh cheese, which is made from yoghurt. It's hot, cool, fresh and spicy all at once.

SAMPHIRE

In South Africa, this sea vegetable grows along the coast and in saltwater marshlands. Thankfully, due to its increasing popularity with chefs, it's now cultivated in the Western Cape. Once referred to as poor-man's asparagus, samphire is both sweet and lip-puckeringly salty, but equally aromatic, pungent and slightly medicinal. South African samphire has thicker, woodier stems than its European counterpart and a crisp, juicy texture. It's a good idea to soak the stems in cold water for at least half an hour prior to cooking, to leach out some of the salt. I like it best simply blanched for a few minutes and dressed in lemon juice, olive oil and cracked black pepper. Mind you hold the salt!

SORREL

Wild sorrel or *suurings* is one of the earliest ingredients used in Cape cooking. The legendary Louis Leipoldt wrote that 'Cape cookery would not be what it should without it'. Some wild sorrels are coarse-leaved and bitter and benefit from cooking, while others are soft with a sweet lemony zing, adding an intriguing element to salads. Sorrel can be used in potato-based soups, gives an interesting twist to tarts or fritters, and can be chopped and mixed into salads. However you choose to use it, sorrel has that distinctive tang: a mouth-puckering acidity that teases and tickles.

WILD GARLIC

In springtime and throughout summer wild garlic grows prolifically in South Africa, its pretty flowers swaying in the breeze like bluebells perched atop slender grassy stalks. It is also cultivated en masse and can be found at just about any nursery countrywide. The flowers are the best part, although the stalks are also edible – if somewhat grassy, with a strong peppery taste – and can be added to pasta, casseroles and risotto. The flowers are so pretty it seems a waste not to use them, which is why one of my favourite dishes is a pile of creamy scrambled eggs on sourdough toast topped with wild garlic flowers.

Pine Ring Frittata

This is a recipe handed to me by a chef friend, Jonathan Japha, after we went mushroom hunting together. The frittata takes on a brilliant orange hue from the pine ring mushrooms, which taste earthy and robust.

5 free-range eggs, beaten
½ cup (125 ml) cream
sea salt
freshly ground black pepper
150 g pine ring mushrooms, cleaned
  of grit and pine needles
2 cloves garlic, peeled and grated
2 Tbs (60 g) butter
1 handful fresh parsley
6 – 8 fresh thyme sprigs

SERVES 2 – 4

In a mixing bowl, whisk the eggs and cream together until well combined. Season and set aside.

Try to use a stovetop-to-oven saucepan for this recipe. In the saucepan, sauté the mushrooms and garlic in the butter until the mushrooms are soft and all the excess moisture has been cooked out (to achieve this, cook over a high heat). Season and add the herbs and egg mixture.

Shimmy the pan gently to make sure the egg mix gets into all the gaps, then immediately turn down the heat.

Place a few knobs of butter at the very edge of the pan and allow them to melt down between the pan and the frittata – this will help to get it out later. Place into the oven. It's ready once the egg is set and cooked through but still moist, about 15 minutes. (But watch it!) You want a slight wobble in the centre.

Once cooked, gently slide it onto a serving plate. It tastes just as good at room temperature as it does fresh from the oven.

CAUTION: *Make sure that you get your wild mushrooms from a trusted source and never, ever forage for mushrooms without an experienced guide. When it comes to pine ring mushrooms, be warned that the similarly coloured Copper Trumpet is deadly poisonous.*

Wild Garlic Flowers with Scrambled Eggs

Usually the leaves of wild garlic are used in cooking in much the same way as one would prepare spinach. I prefer to use the fresh flowers in salads and with eggs. The blooms have a raw, peppery flavour with a potent garlic punch. This is the very best way to make scrambled eggs – the result is always soft and creamy – just as it should be.

1 bunch wild garlic flowers
2 Tbs (60 g) butter
6 eggs
4 Tbs (60 ml) cream
sea salt and cracked black pepper
sourdough toast

SERVES 2

Pick the wild garlic flowers from the stems and give them a rinse, making sure you get rid of any grit. Set aside.

Melt the butter in a non-stick pan. Whisk the eggs very well using a balloon whisk. Add the cream and whisk some more.

Add the eggs to the pan and turn the heat down to medium. Don't stir until the bottom starts to set (as though you were making an omelette), then fold gently rather than stirring the eggs. Leave to settle and firm up between 'folding'. Season with salt and pepper. (I like to season my eggs after they have cooked as I find the scramble to be much softer than when salt is added at the beginning.)

In the meantime, make sure that your bread is toasting as you want to remove the eggs from the pan as soon as they are cooked. I find scrambled eggs are best removed from the heat just before you are happy with the texture, as they tend to continue cooking at a rapid rate. (I like mine very soft.)

Pile onto toast and garnish liberally with wild garlic flowers. The colours are fantastic.

Porcini in Shallot and Brandy Cream

This is a delicious breakfast or brunch dish to follow a late afternoon or evening of foraging for mushrooms.

200 g porcini mushrooms

2 shallots, or 1 medium-sized red
  onion if you can't get shallots,
  finely sliced

2 cloves garlic, finely chopped

3 sprigs of thyme

2 Tbs (60 g) butter

3 Tbs (45 ml) brandy

2 Tbs mascarpone

zest of ½ lemon

sourdough bread, for toasting

thyme sprigs, to serve

SERVES 4

Sauté the mushrooms, shallots, garlic and thyme in the butter until the onions are translucent but not yet browned; about 5 minutes.

Add the brandy, bring to the boil to cook off the alcohol and reduce by about half.

Add the mascarpone and lemon zest, and simmer until thickened and creamy, about 2 minutes.

While the sauce is cooking, toast the sourdough. To serve, place 2 pieces of sourdough toast on individual plates, top with the mushrooms and a sprig or two of thyme and serve immediately.

CAUTION: *Make sure that you get your wild mushrooms from a trusted source and never, ever forage for mushrooms without an experienced guide.*

Sorrel Rosti with Mushrooms and Poached Eggs

This is a version of Eggs Benedict. Sorrel and potato is an excellent combination and the two work particularly well in a rosti.

SORREL ROSTI
5 potatoes, grated
1 large handful or bunch of sorrel,
  finely chopped
½ onion, finely diced
2 cups (240 g) flour
5 eggs
sea salt and ground black pepper
oil, for frying

SPEEDY HOLLANDAISE
1 egg
1 Tbs (15 ml) vinegar
1 Tbs (15 ml) lemon juice
500 g butter

MUSHROOMS
200 g mixed cultivated mushrooms
2 Tbs (60 g) butter

POACHED EGGS
12 eggs
2 Tbs (30 ml) white wine vinegar

SERVES 6

To make the rosti, mix all the ingredients in a large mixing bowl until combined. Form balls of rosti in the palms of your hands and flatten to the size of a small saucer about 1 cm thick.

Heat a little oil in a pan and cook each rosti for about 3 minutes a side, or until golden. Place on paper towels to drain any excess oil. Place on a roasting dish in a warming drawer or very low oven to keep warm.

To make the Hollandaise, place the egg, vinegar and lemon juice in a blender or food processor and blend well.

Heat the butter in the microwave until piping hot (it must be 'foaming' hot). With the motor of the blender running, pour the hot butter into the blender in a slow and steady stream until the sauce begins to thicken. Once it has thickened you can pour all the rest of the butter in and continue to blend until combined. Set aside. (Do not make the Hollandaise ahead or put it in the fridge – it will separate!)

Sauté the mushrooms in the butter until softened. Set aside.

To poach the eggs, place about 4 cm of water in a deep-sided saucepan or pot. Bring to the boil and add the vinegar. Stir the water to make a whirlpool, then crack in the eggs one after the other. (Don't overcrowd the pot by cooking more than four eggs at a time). Cook to your liking (I like my poached eggs soft) and remove with a slotted spoon.

To assemble, place one rosti on each plate. Spoon over a generous amount of mushrooms and top with two poached eggs per plate. Top with Hollandaise and serve.

Wild Mushroom Soup

This is a rich, beautiful dish of porcini soup peppered with thyme and a swirl of cream. You could add any edible foraged mushrooms together with the porcini, but the silkiness of the porcini is most certainly the star.

2 Tbs (30 ml) oil
2 Tbs (60 g) butter
1 onion, finely sliced
500 g fresh porcini, sliced
2 cloves garlic, finely chopped
4 – 6 thyme sprigs
zest of ½ lemon
4 Tbs (60 ml) white wine
2 potatoes, peeled and sliced
2 cups (500 ml) vegetable stock,
  preferably homemade
½ cup (125 ml) cream
sea salt
freshly ground black pepper

SERVES 4

Heat the oil and butter in a non-stick pan and sauté the onion slices until softened. Add the mushrooms and sauté for another minute or two before adding the garlic and thyme. Add the lemon zest and white wine, and reduce until it is almost all evaporated. Set aside.

Place the potatoes in a pot and pour in the stock. Bring to the boil and simmer until the potatoes have softened, about 20 minutes. Add the mushrooms and simmer for another minute or two. Blend using a food processor or hand blender.

When you are ready to serve, add the cream, season and heat through. Serve with crusty French bread.

CAUTION: *Make sure that you get your wild mushrooms from a trusted source and never, ever forage for mushrooms without an experienced guide.*

Nettle and Potato Soup with Crème Fraîche

Stinging nettles are easily tamed by turning them into a wholesome bowl of soup. Boiling the nettles removes the sting, but be sure to wear gloves when handling nettles prior to cooking. Making a soup from nettles is the best way to discover the flavour, simple and unadorned. You'll be surprised by how delicious a bowl of weeds can be.

1 onion, finely sliced
2 leeks, finely sliced
2 cloves garlic
2 Tbs (60 g) butter
5 potatoes, peeled and roughly chopped
3 cups (750 ml) vegetable stock, preferably homemade
2 handfuls stinging nettles
sea salt and ground black pepper
4 Tbs (60 ml) crème fraîche

SERVES 6

In a large pot, sauté the onion, leeks and garlic in the butter until the onion is translucent but not yet browned. Add the potatoes and give it a stir before adding the vegetable stock.

Bring to the boil and simmer until the potatoes are soft. Add the nettles and simmer for a further 5 to 10 minutes or until the nettles have wilted. Remove from the heat and blend using a hand blender or food processor. Season, to taste.

Place the soup back on the heat, add the crème fraîche, and bring back to a gentle simmer to heat through. Serve immediately.

Cucumber Carpaccio with Chilli, Labneh and Purslane

Labneh is a kind of cheese made from yoghurt. It's dead easy to make and delicious. This dish has a surprising layering of flavours – crisp cucumber, hot chillies, cool labneh and succulent, squeaky purslane. Note that you will have to start the labneh the day before.

LABNEH
250 g Greek yoghurt
2 cloves garlic
generous pinch of salt

MARINADE
2 cups (500 ml) white wine vinegar
1 cup (250 ml) tepid water
2 cups (500 ml) olive oil
2 Tbs (30 ml) coriander seeds
4 cloves garlic, whole
2 chillies, whole
2 Tbs (30 ml) dried mixed herbs

CUCUMBER CARPACCIO
1 large cucumber
2 red chillies, deseeded, sliced
200 g purslane leaves, picked off
  the stems
extra virgin olive oil, for serving

SERVES 4

Make the labneh a day or two ahead. Line a sieve with muslin or cheesecloth. Place the lined sieve over a bowl and pour the yoghurt into the sieve. Refrigerate overnight. The more time you give the yoghurt to drain, the firmer the cheese.

The following day, the yoghurt will have lost any excess moisture and firmed up to the texture of cottage cheese. Press down on the yoghurt in the sieve to release any excess moisture, before tumbling it into a clean bowl. Grate the garlic into the yoghurt and add the salt. Mash it all together, cover and return to the fridge until required.

To make the marinade, mix all the ingredients together and set aside till required.

To make the carpaccio, peel long strips of cucumber by shaving it lengthwise with a potato peeler. Place the strips of cucumber into the marinade in a deep bowl, cover and refrigerate for a couple of hours or overnight.

To serve, remove as many strips of cucumber as you need from the marinade and arrange onto serving plates. Place a large dollop of labneh in the centre of each plate on top of the cucumber, scatter over the chilli and purslane, and drizzle generously with olive oil.

Warm Salad of Samphire, Asparagus and Pine Nuts

It makes perfect sense that sea asparagus (samphire) be used with green asparagus – the two were made for each other. The addition of lemon and farm-fresh butter with toasted pine nuts rounds it off beautifully. Be sure to hold the salt though.

300 g samphire
1 large bunch asparagus
100 g unsalted butter
juice and zest of 1 lemon
½ cup (75 g) toasted pine nuts

SERVES 4 AS A STARTER

Trim away any woody stalks from the samphire and the asparagus. Bring a large pot of water to the boil (do not salt, as samphire is particularly salty) and add the asparagus. Cook for 2 minutes, then add the samphire and cook for another minute. Strain and cool under cold running water to stop the asparagus from going limp.

Divide evenly amongst four plates or place on a platter. Melt the butter and add the lemon juice and zest. Drizzle over the asparagus and samphire, then add the toasted pine nuts.

Serve immediately, whilst warm.

CHAPTER 6

Local Heroes

With all the beautiful produce available these days, it's easy to miss the small things that are right in front of us – not only ingredients grown on home soil, but produce that is truly South African in every way. Things like mielies – and I'm not talking about sweetcorn, but true South African heirloom maize varieties such as Transkei Flint Corn and the aptly named Golden Beauty (*see* A Note on Heirlooms on page 11). And what about *hereboontjies* and *goeweneursboontjies*, our very own version of lima beans?

These dried beans are in serious danger of extinction, as they have a low yield, producing an average of only two beans per pod. Both are found along the West Coast and inland towards the Sandveld. Not surprisingly, farmers are quickly losing interest in planting them. *Goeweneursboontjies* (governor's beans) are large, flat white types, whereas the creamy, thin-skinned *hereboontjies* (gentleman's beans) are butter yellow or white.

Then there's the *wit boerpampoen,* our very own, enormous, home-grown pumpkin. My earliest memory of the 'Wit boer' is of rows and rows of huge, flat white pumpkins stored on the rooftops of outbuildings on our Karoo farm – a familiar sight if you're ever travelling past rural *dorpies* in wintertime.

Morogo, also known as wild or African spinach, is another typical staple ingredient of our country. *Morogo* technically refers to a group of at least three different dark leafy green vegetables found in southern Africa. Traditionally cooked in stews, *morogo* can be prepared in much the same way as Swiss chard, but benefits from the added flavour from ingredients such as garlic, lemon, butter and onions. One of my favourite recipes, found in these pages, is a soup-stew of *hereboontjies*, *morogo* and garlic cooked in the same fashion as a traditional Italian bread soup, with hunks of day-old bread used to thicken the sauce. A generous amount of Parmesan and a drizzling of grassy olive oil rounds it off beautifully.

Technically not vegetables at all, *suurvygies* (sour figs) and *waterblommetjies* have sustained generations and are renowned as *veldkos* or field 'vegetables'. *Waterblommetjies* are also referred to as *wateruintjies* or water onions. Both of these grow in the wild. Naturally sun-dried *suurvygies* are mostly eaten *in situ*, the tips chewed off and discarded, and the jammy flesh sucked from its leathery skin. *Waterblommetjies*, best known as the star ingredient in a lamb bredie, need some attention in the form of stewing or pickling, but they do also make good additions to vegetable soup.

Hereboontjies

Hereboontjies are South Africa's very own oversized lima bean and have a very long history in the Western Cape. Only grown in certain parts of the Cape, *hereboontjies* were named after Jan van Riebeek, '*Die Heer van die Kaap*' (the Lord of the Cape). The story goes that Van Riebeek shipped these white beans over to the Queen, as they were the only beans she would eat. *Hereboontjies* are mostly found dried and are delicious served in casseroles and soup. Head up the West Coast and towards the Sandveld area and you'll no doubt find them in tiny supermarkets and roadside farm stalls.

Mielies

Mielies are synonymous with South African cooking, whether it be for survival in the form of samp (dried corn kernels) or mielie meal, or for pure pleasure. There is a small selection of old South African heirloom varieties and the few people who save the seeds year after year are helping to keep the diminishing seed resource from extinction. Transkei Flint Corn and Golden Beauty (aptly named for its striking burnt yellow, almost orange colour) are two such varieties. If you can see past the simple pleasure of serving corn on the cob, there are a multitude of recipes using mielies; pan-fried fritters served with grilled banana, dripping with crimson prickly pear syrup; mielie bread with the mildest hint of chilli and mature cheddar; or a delicious smoky corn chowder.

Morogo

Also known as African spinach, *morogo* is a leafy green that grows prolifically in the wild and forms part of the staple diet in Africa. My great-aunt Eve Palmer was often spotted scouring the roadside verges outside her home in Pretoria for *morogo*. 'I remember an African woman who used to pick *morogo* along our pavement,' she said, 'now I am surely the only one who hunts it along the sidewalks of Waterkloof!' Likened to Swiss chard, it can be cooked in much the same way: steamed, boiled, sautéed or added to soups and casseroles.

SUURVYGIES

A mat-forming succulent, *suurvygies* (*Carpobrotus edulis*) or sour figs are found mostly along the South African coastline. They dry out naturally in the sun and, once picked, the tip can be snipped (or more likely chewed off) and the jammy flesh inside sucked or squeezed out and eaten. In summertime *suurvygies* are plentiful and can be bought by the bagful in tiny coastal towns. They make a vibrant crimson-coloured jam (if you can bear not to eat them all at once) that is just made to share a plate with a wedge of sharp cheese and farm-baked bread.

WATERBLOMMETJIES

For too long now, *waterblommetjies* have been associated with *bredie* – a traditional lamb stew with *waterblommetjies* as the star ingredient. Also known as Cape pondweed, *waterblommetjies* (*Aponogeton distachyos*) are native to the Western Cape of South Africa and can be found in ponds, marshes and wetlands in the wintertime. Best eaten in bud-phase, there's more to the *waterblommetjie* than *bredie*. Pickle the buds and serve with cheese, chop the sweet-smelling flowers of the first tender *blommetjies* and add to salads, or steam and stir into a lemon risotto. It's time the humble *waterblommetjie* got the treatment it truly deserves as a local hero.

WIT BOERPAMPOEN

A few years ago, this truly South African pumpkin was the most common variety sold as a seed throughout the country. Unfortunately it is slowly being replaced by new hybrids found in nurseries across the country. Now, more than ever, we should be saving the seeds of our heritage (*see* A Note on Heirlooms on page 11). The flesh, texture and flavour of the *boerpampoen* is far superior to most pumpkins I've tried and lends itself to all manner of dishes from cinnamon-sweet fritters to golden, honey-roasted wedges.

Mielie Bread with Chilli

This is one of my favourite bread recipes, as it is so easy, moist and delicious.

1 cup (250 ml) finely sliced onions
4 Tbs (120 g) butter
1 red chilli, deseeded and finely
  chopped
1 tsp (5 ml) dried mixed herbs
2 Tbs (30 ml) parsley, finely chopped
2 cups (300 g) fresh mielie kernels
  (you can use a can of mielie
  kernels instead)
1 cup (150 g) grated carrot
1 cup (100 g) grated cheddar
2½ cups (300 g) flour
2 tsp (10 ml) baking powder
1 tsp (5 ml) salt
1 tub (250 g) yoghurt
3 eggs, whisked

SERVES 6

Sauté the onions in the butter, add the chilli and mixed herbs, stirring until the onion has softened, then set aside to cool.

To a large mixing bowl, add the parsley, mielie kernels, carrot, cheddar, and the onion and herb mix.

In a separate mixing bowl, sift the flour, baking powder and salt. Sift twice, then add to the vegetable mix. (You can do the second sift directly into the bowl with the vegetables, sifting over the mix.)

In a bowl, combine the yoghurt and eggs, then add to the vegetable mix.

Pour into a small loaf tin and bake in a preheated oven at 200 °C for 1½ hours. Turn the oven off and leave the loaf in the oven until the oven cools, by which time the bread should be perfect.

Spicy Mielie Chowder with Avocado Salsa

The avocado salsa rounds this chowder off beautifully and is so worth making. To finish it off, I like to serve this soup with large corn nachos-type crisps or toasted tortilla wedges (simply place under the grill until toasted).

SPICY MIELIE CHOWDER
2 onions, chopped
2 carrots, diced
1 Tbs (15 ml) olive oil
1 Tbs (30 g) butter
1 tsp (5 ml) cayenne pepper
1 tsp (5 ml) smoked paprika
fresh mielie kernels from 4 cobs
3 medium sweet potatoes, peeled
  and cubed
4 cups (1 litre) vegetable stock,
  preferably homemade
sea salt and black pepper
crème fraîche, to serve

AVOCADO SALSA
2 ripe avocados, diced into about
  1 cm cubes
1 tomato, diced
1 red chilli, deseeded, finely sliced
1 handful fresh coriander, finely
  sliced
4 spring onions, finely sliced
juice of ½ lemon
4 Tbs (60 ml) extra virgin olive oil
sea salt
black pepper

SERVES 6

For the soup, sauté the onions and carrots in the oil and butter until the onions are translucent, but not yet brown. Add the cayenne pepper, paprika and mielie kernels, and stir for about a minute to develop the flavours.

Add the sweet potato and pour in enough stock to just cover the vegetables. Bring to the boil, then simmer for about 25 to 30 minutes or until the sweet potato is soft and tender.

Using a hand blender, blend the soup, but not to a purée. I like to serve this soup fairly chunky, so blend only part of it. Season, to taste.

For the avocado salsa, combine all the ingredients in a bowl, season and toss together.

To serve, heat the soup, ladle into bowls, garnish with a spoon of crème fraîche and a dollop of salsa. Serve with toasted tortilla or corn chips.

Soup-stew of Hereboontjies, Morogo and Garlic

This is a classic bread soup, which is more a meal than a soup, really. Packed with flavour it's beautifully finished off with a generous drizzle of good olive oil just before eating.

350 g dried hereboontjies
1 onion, finely sliced
2 Tbs (30 ml) olive oil, plus extra
   for serving
4 cloves garlic, finely chopped
2 dried bird's eye chillies, finely
   sliced
leaves from 3 rosemary sprigs, finely
   chopped
2 x 410 g cans whole peeled
   tomatoes
sea salt and cracked black pepper
3 cups (750 ml) vegetable stock,
   preferably homemade
300 g morogo, roughly chopped,
   stalks removed
4 thick slices day-old ciabatta
1 handful grated Parmesan

SERVES 4

Soak the *hereboontjies* for at least 5 hours, or preferably overnight. Drain, then cook in fresh boiling water for about 1 hour or until the beans are soft. (Note: do not add salt to the boiling water, as the beans will toughen.)

While the beans are cooking, sauté the onion in the olive oil until translucent, then add the garlic, chilli and rosemary, stirring for about 1 minute. Add the tomatoes, stirring to break them up, and season.

Simmer for about 10 minutes to reduce slightly then add the cooked, drained *hereboontjies* and stock. Bring back to the boil then add the *morogo*. Simmer for about 15 minutes, or until the *morogo* is soft.

Break the bread into pieces and stir into the pot with the Parmesan. Turn the heat down to low and simmer until the bread has absorbed the beautiful flavours and is meltingly soft, about 5 to 10 minutes. The soup should be flavourful and thick.

Ladle into soup bowls, drizzle with olive oil and serve.

Waterblommetjie Quiche with Cheese Pastry

I first discovered a version of this recipe through Cape cooking doyenne Judy Badenhorst. Judy adds Brie to her waterblommetjie quiche, which makes it creamy and delicious. I've opted for a simple Parmesan and waterblom quiche, which is beautifully offset with the lemon.

CHEESE PASTRY

2 cups (200 g) grated cheddar
  cheese
180 g butter
2 cups (240 g) cake flour
a pinch cayenne pepper

QUICHE FILLING

750 g waterblommetjies, ends cut
  and halved lengthwise, rinsed
zest of 1 lemon
juice of ½ lemon
sea salt and pepper
2 cups (500 ml) cream
5 eggs
½ cup (60 g) grated Parmesan
extra Parmesan, for sprinkling

MAKES 1 MEDIUM-SIZED QUICHE

Place all the ingredients for the cheese pastry in a food processor and blend to form a loose ball. Press into a 22 cm-diameter loose-bottomed tart tin and place in the freezer for about 15 to 20 minutes.

Line the inside of the tart with greaseproof paper, fill with dried beans, and blind bake in a preheated oven at 180 °C for 20 minutes. Remove from the oven, discard the paper and beans, and set aside.

To make the filling, bring a saucepan of water to the boil and cook the *waterblommetjies* until tender, but still holding their shape; about 20 minutes. Place the tender *waterblommetjies* into the bowl of a food processor (reserving 1 cup of florets to decorate the quiche) with the lemon zest and juice, and blend until smooth. Season to taste.

Mix in 1 cup (250 ml) cream, and spoon the *waterblommetjie* purée into the prepared tart case.

In a bowl, beat the eggs, the remaining cream and Parmesan together. Season to taste. Pour the mixture over the *waterblommetjie* purée and decorate with the reserved florets.

Sprinkle with some extra Parmesan and bake in a preheated oven at 180 °C for 40 minutes or until golden. Serve warm.

Roast Boerpampoen with Crispy Breadcrumbs

This is a delicious way to serve boerpampoen, as the zesty breadcrumbs add texture to sticky roasted pumpkin.

750 g boerpampoen, peeled, seeded
   and cubed
2 Tbs (60 g) butter
sea salt and black pepper
2 cloves garlic, peeled and
   finely chopped
1 red chilli, deseeded and
   finely chopped
4 Tbs (60 ml) oil
2 sprigs rosemary, leaves removed,
   finely chopped
zest of 1 orange
1 handful parsley, finely chopped
2 cups (120 g) fresh breadcrumbs

SERVES 4 – 6 AS A SIDE DISH

Steam the pumpkin for 20 to 25 minutes, or until tender. Tumble into a roasting dish, add the butter, season and set aside.

Sauté the garlic and chilli in the oil for about 2 minutes. Add the rosemary, orange zest, parsley and breadcrumbs, and stir over a low to medium heat, until the breadcrumbs are golden. Pour the breadcrumb mix over the pumpkin, season, drizzle with olive oil and bake in a preheated oven at 180 °C for 25 to 30 minutes.

Best Boerpampoen Fritters

I love pumpkin fritters. Traditionally the batter is sweetened with sugar, but I prefer mine without the addition of sugar prior to cooking – just a light dusting of cinnamon sugar to serve.

500 g pumpkin, cut into cubes
¼ cup (60 ml) water
½ cup (60 g) all-purpose flour
½ tsp (3 ml) salt
1 tsp (5 ml) ground cinnamon
2 tsp (10 ml) baking powder
2 eggs
vegetable oil for frying
cinnamon sugar, for dusting

MAKES ABOUT 15 FRITTERS

Pumpkin holds a lot of water, so it is essential that the cooked pumpkin is dry. To do this, cook the pumpkin over a low heat, with the lid of the pot removed, in a tiny bit of water, ¼ cup (60 ml) should do it. Alternatively, steam.

Once the pumpkin is cooked, mash it well with a fork. You will need only 2 cups of mashed pumpkin to make the fritters. Add to a food processor along with the rest of the ingredients, except for the eggs, vegetable oil and cinnamon sugar. (You can mix it by hand, but the processor works like a dream.) Once the dry ingredients are combined, add the eggs and process to form a thick batter.

Heat enough oil in a pot or deep-sided pan to shallow-fry the fritters. Drop heaped tablespoons of the batter into the oil and fry until golden on both sides. Remove and drain on paper towels. Dust with cinnamon sugar and serve.

Mielie Fritters with Grilled Bananas

There is nothing quite like a mielie fritter for breakfast, especially if it's dripping with prickly pear syrup. This vibrant crimson syrup can be found at farm stalls, or you could make it yourself (find a fool-proof recipe in my first book, aptly named Prickly Pears & Pomegranates). *If that all seems too much effort, maple syrup will do the trick.*

2 cups (300 g) mielie kernels, fresh or canned
3 spring onions, finely sliced
1 small handful coriander, finely chopped
1 small handful parsley, finely chopped
1 cup (120 g) plain flour
1 tsp (5 ml) baking powder
a pinch salt
½ tsp (3 ml) paprika
1 Tbs (15 ml) sugar
2 eggs
½ cup (125 ml) milk
4 Tbs (60 ml) vegetable oil
4 bananas, halved lengthwise
8 Tbs (125 g) mascarpone
prickly pear syrup, to serve

SERVES 4

If using fresh mielie kernels, steam for 10 to 15 minutes. Once cooled, place in a mixing bowl together with the spring onions and herbs. Set aside.

Sift the flour, baking powder, salt and paprika into a large mixing bowl. Add the sugar, and give it a stir to combine.

In a separate bowl, whisk together the eggs and milk. Slowly add the egg mix to the dry ingredients, whisking continuously until smooth. The batter should be smooth and lump-free. Add the batter to the corn mixture to bind. (Note: do not add the batter to the vegetables more than an hour before cooking or the batter will become watery.)

To cook the fritters, fry about 2 tablespoons (30 ml) of batter at a time over a medium heat until golden, about 2 minutes a side. Keep warm until all the fritters have been cooked.

In the meantime, grill the bananas in a pan over a low heat.

To serve, place one fritter on a plate, top with two banana halves, a dollop of mascarpone and a generous drizzle of prickly pear syrup. Finish with a second fritter on top, another dollop of mascarpone and drizzle some more prickly pear syrup around the base of the stack. Serve immediately.

OPPOSITE: *Heirloom corn (from left): Golden Beauty, Blue Aztec, Transkei Flint Corn, Red Maize*

Suurvygie Jam

I first stumbled upon this jam on the roadside at the top of Constantia Nek a few years ago and was intrigued. I had only ever experienced suurvygies, as a child, picked near the dunes at my Ouma's beach house in the Western Cape. You make it as you would most any jam, using equal amounts of sugar and fruit, but the best thing about this jam is the colour – it turns an unexpected deep shade of red.

700 g dried suurvygies
700 g sugar
4 cups (1 litre) water
2 Tbs (30 ml) fresh lemon juice
thumb of fresh ginger, grated
4 whole cloves

MAKES 4 JARS

Place whole *suurvygies* in a large bowl, pour over enough tepid water to cover, and leave to soak overnight. Cut off the hard bit at the bottom of each *suurvygie* – where the stem was attached to the base – and discard.

Place the *suurvygies* in a large pot, cover with water, bring to the boil and simmer until tender, about 45 minutes. Drain and set aside.

In a clean pot, bring the sugar and water to the boil, stirring, making sure that the sugar dissolves before the water starts to boil. Add the *suurvygies*, lemon juice, ginger and cloves. Boil until the syrup is thick enough to coat the back of a spoon, about 30 minutes.

Pour into sterilised jars, seal and label.

OVERLEAF: *Suurvygies*

CHAPTER 7

Grains & Pulses

What would a book on vegetables be without grains? Of course they're not vegetables. But the two do go hand in hand. Grains and pulses form the backbone of every pantry and appear in many different guises. The beauty is that they have a tremendous ability to absorb flavour, so benefit from cooking with spices, herbs and garlic – or a flavourful homemade stock. Dress them whilst hot with a grassy extra virgin olive oil, zesty lemon, a smattering of Parmesan and chopped herbs, and once they've cooled you'll have the makings of a delicious salad. Mix in a couple of chunks of marinated aubergine or roasted beetroot and it will be a dish that's hard to resist.

Pulses are available all year round – whether fresh or dried – and most benefit from soaking in cold water for a couple of hours. The golden rule when cooking with pulses is never to add salt until they are soft, as salt toughens the skins.

BARLEY

Ceres, the Roman goddess of fertility and the harvest, wears a crown of plaited barley on her head. The Greeks have loved barley for centuries – they use it for flat bread as its low gluten content prevents the dough from rising. Pearl barley is indispensable in the pantry and is incredibly versatile. Use it in a chunky vegetable soup; as a substitute for Arborio in a richly nutritious and comforting risotto; in a salad with chopped, fresh mint, garden peas and spring broad beans; or as an accompaniment to casseroles and stews. Barley lends an earthy wholesomeness to a dish that is somehow missing in rice, couscous or quinoa.

CHICKPEAS

It's so easy to buy chickpeas in a can, but do consider buying them dried and cooking them at home. They have a certain texture that is lost in the canned version. However, canned chickpeas are a store-cupboard necessity as they can be used in all types of dishes for last-minute entertaining: blend with fresh garlic, lemon juice and a pinch of cumin for a delicious hummus; rinse and toss together with red onion strips, chopped fresh chilli, coriander, mint and baby tomatoes for a quick side dish; or mix with couscous, chopped herbs and roasted peppers. And next time – when you have the time to plan ahead – use dried chickpeas, soak them overnight and use as desired.

COUSCOUS

Steaming, fluffy couscous with a pinch of salt flakes and a melting knob of butter dripping through the granules makes a great alternative to rice – and even mash. A traditional Berber dish of semolina, couscous is a staple food across Tunisia, Morocco and Algeria. Serve it hot to accompany just about any main, or toss together with soft herbs, oven-dried tomatoes and Danish feta. It's a great partner to roast Mediterranean vegetables and comes into its own flecked with raisins or dates and served with a North African vegetable tagine.

KIDNEY BEANS

Of all the pulses in the world – and there are many – kidney beans are a firm favourite. The deep red, glossy skins bring any dish to life and add texture and colour. Kidney beans go very well with eggs and one of the best ways to prepare the two is to make a spicy stew of tomatoes, beans and chillies and top with soft poached eggs and fresh coriander. Raw kidney beans, also called chilli beans or red beans, must be boiled for at least 10 minutes prior to any form of cooking to destroy toxins commonly found in the bean in its raw state.

LENTILS

The beauty about lentils, especially for vegetarians, is that – when cooked in the right manner – they add an element of meatiness to any dish. Consider a bubbling lentil cottage pie with golden butternut, carrots and tomatoes topped with buttery mashed sweet potato and a grating of strong cheddar. Who needs meat? There are so many types, from the coveted Puy lentil to the brown, green, black and red varieties. One of my favourite dishes is an aromatic Indian dhal served with flat bread or roti – best eaten messily by using the bread to scoop up the spicy mix. Lentils are just as good in soups,

casseroles or added to salads with roast beetroot and goat's cheese.

QUINOA

Quinoa is the ultimate power food. A grain-like crop originating high up in the Andes in Peru, it's packed with protein. There is a vast range of possibilities when it comes to serving quinoa: it makes a tasty high-protein breakfast mixed with honey, almonds and berries; or serve it as a substitute to couscous or rice, with a spoonful of zesty salsa verde; or in a salad with mixed sprouts and micro leaves. Red quinoa is a particularly striking ingredient tossed with herbs in a modern take on tabbouleh and served on a stark white platter for contrast.

RICE

Rice has transformed landscapes around the world with vast expanses of paddy fields dotted with temples dedicated to rice deities, and has fed the most populated nations across the globe. Brown rice, wild rice, Arborio, basmati, jasmine and black rice each have their own unique qualities that make them best-suited to certain types of dishes. Black sticky rice is naturally sweet and dark and makes for a striking bowl of rice pudding for dessert; brown rice is unrivalled in a nutritious pilaf of toasted nuts, spinach and crumbly Greek feta; jasmine rice has the fragrance that is so characteristically suited to Thai food; Arborio has the absorption needed for risottos; and basmati is the choice for Indian cooking. Little wonder that rice rivals wheat as the world's most important food crop.

Red Quinoa, Avocado and Broccoli Power Salad

This is a salad that's been on the Café Roux menu since we first opened, and it remains a local favourite. Quinoa is packed with goodness, and the creaminess of Danish feta and avocado is perfectly offset by the crunch of sprouts.

POWER SALAD

1 cup (200 g) uncooked red quinoa
2 handfuls watercress
2 cups broccoli florets, blanched
1 avocado, sliced
½ cup (75 g) sunflower seeds,
  toasted
½ cup (75 g) pumpkin seeds, toasted
Danish feta, broken into chunks
1 handful onion sprouts

HERB VINAIGRETTE

4 cloves garlic, crushed
1 cup (250 ml) white wine vinegar
1 handful fresh coriander
1 handful fresh mint
2 Tbs (75 g) white sugar
1 cup (250 ml) extra virgin olive oil
½ cup (125 ml) vegetable oil

SERVES 6

Bring a large pot of water to the boil. Add the quinoa and cook for about 20 minutes, or until the grains start to split and turn slightly transparent. Drain and set aside to cool.

In the meantime, make the dressing. Using a hand blender, blend all the ingredients together, except for the oil. Stir in the oil gently and set aside.

Once the quinoa has cooled sufficiently, toss together with the watercress in a large bowl. Either arrange on a platter or divide evenly amongst four salad plates. Top with blanched broccoli, avocado slices, toasted seeds, some feta and, finally, the onion sprouts.

Dress only once you are ready to serve or the seeds will go soggy.

Baked Kidney Beans with Chilli and Poached Eggs

This is the kind of dish you could largely put together the night before a brunch and all that's required on the day is cracking a couple of eggs and placing the dish in the oven. The eggs are poached in the spicy tomato sauce.

225 g dried red kidney beans
   or 1 can (400 g) kidney beans,
   drained and rinsed
8 large, free-range eggs

TOMATO-CHILLI SAUCE
1 onion, finely sliced
2 Tbs (15 ml) olive oil
2 cloves garlic, finely sliced
1 red chilli, deseeded and finely
   sliced
1 tsp smoked paprika
200 g Rosa or cherry tomatoes
2 x 400 g cans whole baby tomatoes
salt, to taste
black pepper, to taste
1 handful parsley, finely chopped
1 handful basil, finely chopped
Danish feta, to serve (optional)

SERVES 4

Soak the dried kidney beans overnight. Strain, then add to a pot of fresh water. Bring to the boil and simmer for about 1 hour or until the beans are soft. Strain and set aside.

In a deep-sided casserole, sauté the onion in the oil until translucent, but not yet golden. Add the garlic, chilli and smoked paprika, and continue cooking for about 2 minutes, stirring. Add the fresh and canned tomatoes, season, bring to the boil and simmer for 20 minutes.

Add the kidney beans, parsley and basil, and simmer for a further 5 minutes.

Now you can either crack all the eggs into the casserole on top of the tomato-chilli or you could ladle the tomato chilli into individual serving-sized baking dishes or large ramekins, cracking two eggs per dish on top of the tomato chilli sauce.

Place in a preheated oven at 200 °C for about 15 to 20 minutes or until the eggs are baked to your liking.

Top with crumbled feta and serve with crusty bread.

Pearl Barley, Broad Bean and Pea Salad

This is one of my all-time favourite salads. Peas, broad beans, mint and goat's cheese were made to go together and this combination with the pearl barley makes a spectacular salad.

SALAD
1 cup (220 g) pearl barley
1 cup (150 g) peas, fresh or frozen
1 cup (150 g) broad beans
wild rocket
fresh mint, finely chopped
1 log goat's chevin

HERB VINAIGRETTE
4 cloves garlic, crushed
1 cup (250 ml) white wine vinegar
1 handful fresh coriander
1 handful fresh mint
2 Tbs (30 ml) white sugar
1 cup (250 ml) extra virgin olive oil
½ cup (125 ml) vegetable oil

SERVES 4–6

Cook the barley in boiling, salted water until tender. Strain and leave to cool.

In the meantime, make the dressing. Using a hand blender, blend all the ingredients together, except for the oil. Stir in the oil gently and set aside.

Cook the peas in a pot of boiling water for about 10 minutes if using fresh, or 2 minutes if using frozen. In a separate pot, blanch the broad beans until the outer membrane slips off easily. Cool under cold running water and slip off the membrane. Add to the pot with the peas for the last 2 minutes of cooking time.

Toss the rocket, peas, broad beans, mint and pearl barley together, dress, and place on a large platter. Scatter the goat's cheese over the top and serve.

Chilli and Chickpea Salad

This recipe requires a bit of planning, as you'll need to soak the chickpeas overnight. The cool cucumber offsets the heat of the chillies, and the chickpeas add crunch.

CHICKPEA SALAD

450 g dried chickpeas (or 2 cans
  chickpeas, drained and rinsed)
4 Tbs (60 ml) extra virgin olive oil
juice of ½ lemon
sea salt and cracked black pepper
4 plum tomatoes, diced
½ small cucumber, diced
1 handful coriander leaves,
  roughly chopped
1 handful fresh mint, finely chopped
1 handful parsley, finely chopped
1 red chilli, deseeded and
  finely sliced
1 red onion, diced

MUSTARD DRESSING

½ cup (100 g) sugar
2 tsp (10 ml) Dijon mustard
2 tsp (10 ml) salt
⅔ cup (160 ml) white vinegar
2 cups (500 ml) canola oil

SERVES 6 AS A SIDE

Soak the dried chickpeas overnight. Drain and rinse, then bring to the boil in cold water. Do not season or the skins will toughen. Simmer for 1 ½ hours or until the chickpeas are soft, skimming away any scum that rises to the surface.

Drain and dress immediately with the olive oil and lemon juice. Season, to taste. The hot chickpeas will soak up the flavours as they cool.

To make the dressing, whisk all the ingredients together in a mixing bowl until the sugar is dissolved. (You can use olive oil if you prefer, but the fruitiness doesn't work as well with this salad.) This recipe makes at least 3 cups of dressing; remaining dressing can be stored, covered, in the fridge for up to 3 weeks.

Toss all the remaining salad ingredients together with the chickpeas in a large mixing bowl. Dress and tumble into a deep serving bowl.

Harissa Couscous with Sticky Butternut

Harissa is a spicy North African sauce that works beautifully with couscous. This is a meal-in-one kind of dish that could be served for lunch or supper (or as a side dish).

Couscous

1 large butternut, cubed
oil for roasting
sea salt and black pepper
2 cups (400 g) couscous
1 cup (100 g) sun-dried or
  oven-dried tomatoes, sliced
  (*see* page 81)
1 large handful wild rocket

Harissa Paste

4 red peppers, roasted
2 red chillies, deseeded and
  roughly chopped
3 cloves garlic, roughly chopped
1 Tbs (15 ml) ground coriander
1 Tbs (15 ml) ground cumin
2 handfuls fresh coriander
1 cup (250 ml) olive oil
juice of 1 lemon
sea salt and black pepper
1 Tbs (15 ml) sugar

Serves 6

Place the butternut and red peppers (for the harissa) in a roasting dish, drizzle with oil and season. Roast in a preheated oven at 200 °C for about 25 minutes. Set aside the butternut, skin and deseed the roasted peppers and use them for the harissa.

To make the harissa paste, place the roasted red peppers in a food processor together with the rest of the harissa ingredients, and blend to form a sauce.

Place the couscous in a bowl and cover with enough boiling water to just cover the grains. Cover tightly and set aside. Once all the water has been absorbed, separate the grains of couscous using a fork.

Mix the cooked couscous with harissa to taste, stirring well (if you need to thin the harissa paste a little, do so with a bit of boiling water).

Add the sun-dried tomatoes, roasted butternut and rocket, and toss all together. Serve.

Quinoa Tabbouleh with Pomegranate Rubies

Quinoa is now readily available at most health stores and supermarkets countrywide. The colour of this dish is fantastic and the addition of pomegranate seeds makes it extra special and vibrant.

QUINOA TABBOULEH
1 cup (200 g) uncooked quinoa
2 pomegranates
2 handfuls parsley, finely chopped
1 small handful mint, finely chopped
1 handful coriander, finely chopped
½ medium cucumber, diced

POMEGRANATE DRESSING
6 Tbs (90 ml) extra virgin olive oil
3 Tbs (45 ml) freshly squeezed
  lemon juice
1 Tbs (15 ml) pomegranate molasses
1 handful fresh mint, finely chopped
sea salt
freshly ground black pepper

SERVES 4

Cook the quinoa in a pot with lots of boiling water. Simmer for about 20 to 30 minutes, or until the grain begins to split and turn transparent around the edges. Strain and set aside to cool.

Crack open the pomegranates and, working over a mixing bowl, remove the seeds. (The mixing bowl will catch all the juices from the pomegranate, which will be delicious added to the dressing.) Set aside the seeds.

To make the dressing, add the oil, lemon juice and molasses to the mixing bowl containing the pomegranate juice and whisk all together. Add the mint, season to taste, and set aside.

In a large bowl toss together all the tabbouleh ingredients, including the cooled quinoa, dress and serve.

Nutty Pilaf with Black Kale, Walnuts and Feta

Black kale, walnuts and feta is one of my favourite combinations – nutty, salty and nutritious. (You could use spinach or chard instead of the black kale, but the colour is not as dramatic.) It's the sort of recipe where you can add the ingredients to a casserole dish and leave it to tick away in the oven before adding the final touches.

6 – 8 spring onions, finely sliced

3 cloves garlic, finely sliced

1 tsp (5 ml) fennel seeds

2 Tbs (30 ml) olive oil

2 Tbs (60 g) butter

1 ½ cups (300 g) brown basmati rice

juice and zest of 1 lemon

3 cups (750 ml) vegetable stock, preferably homemade

salt and black pepper, to taste

200 g black kale, stalks discarded, leaves shredded

1 handful parsley, finely chopped

100 g walnuts, crushed

2 rounds of feta, crumbled

1 small handful mint, finely chopped

SERVES 6

Sauté the spring onions, garlic and fennel seeds in the oil over a medium heat for about 2 minutes, or to soften. Add the butter and, once melted, add the rice and cook, stirring continuously, for 1 to 2 minutes or until the grains are evenly coated.

Turn up the heat and add the lemon juice and zest. Add the stock, and season to taste. Bring to the boil, then reduce the heat to low, cover and cook for about 30 to 35 minutes, or until all the liquid has been absorbed.

Place the shredded kale and parsley on top of the rice for the last 5 minutes of cooking. Turn off the heat and leave to stand for 10 minutes, before forking through the kale.

Tumble into a serving dish, top with walnuts, feta and mint, and serve.

Mild Chickpea Curry with Toasted Coconut

A great meal-in-one, the toasted coconut adds a crunch to this mildy spiced casserole. Serve on its own or with rice.

400 g dried chickpeas or 2 cans,
    drained and rinsed
2 tsp (10 ml) coriander seeds
2 tsp (10 ml) cumin seeds
1 dried lime leaf
4 cm ginger, grated
2 cloves garlic, finely sliced
2 stems lemon grass, white part
    only, chopped
2 Tbs (30 ml) olive oil
1 large red onion, finely sliced
½ tsp (3 ml) turmeric
1 tsp (5 ml) cayenne pepper
4 large, ripe tomatoes, roughly
    chopped
½ cup (125 ml) vegetable stock,
    preferably homemade
½ can (200 ml) coconut milk
sea salt and ground black pepper
½ cup (50 g) coconut flakes, toasted

SERVES 4

Soak the chickpeas in cold water overnight. Strain and cook in a large pot of boiling water. Do not salt the water or the skins will toughen. Simmer for 45 minutes to 1 hour, or until soft. Strain and set aside.

Using a pestle and mortar, grind the coriander and cumin seeds, and the lime leaf. Add the ginger, garlic and lemon grass and pound to a rough paste.

In a heavy-bottomed casserole, sauté the paste in the oil until the aromas are released; about 2 minutes. Add the onion, turmeric and cayenne pepper, and sauté until just beginning to brown. Add the tomatoes, stirring for another minute or so before adding the stock, coconut milk and chickpeas.

Bring to the boil and simmer for 10 to 15 minutes, reducing slightly, until the tomatoes soften and start breaking up. Adjust the seasoning.

Top with toasted coconut flakes and serve.

Red Lentil and Spinach Dhal

Dhal has to be one of the most comforting – and moreish – dishes around. The coconut milk in this one mellows the heat to a mild warmth. It's delicious spooned into a roti and eaten with your hands.

1¼ cups (250 g) red lentils
1 tsp (5 ml) ground turmeric
sunflower oil
1 tsp (5 ml) cumin seeds
1 tsp (5 ml) mustard seeds
2 onions, finely sliced
3 cm ginger, grated
2 cloves garlic, finely sliced
   or grated
2 dried bird's eye chillies,
   finely sliced
1 bunch spinach, roughly chopped
1 x 400 ml can coconut milk
1 tsp (5 ml) garam masala
salt, to taste
fresh coriander, to serve
chopped chillies, to serve

SERVES 8

Rinse the lentils and soak in cold water for at least 20 minutes. Place the lentils and turmeric in a large pot, pour in enough cold water to cover the lentils, bring to the boil and then simmer until the lentils are tender; about 30 minutes. Strain and set aside.

Heat the oil in a heavy-bottomed saucepan and add the cumin and mustard seeds and cook until they start to pop. Add the onions and sauté until browning slightly. Add the ginger, garlic and dried chillies.

Stir for about 2 minutes, then add the spinach and stir until wilted. Add the coconut milk and lentils and simmer gently for a few minutes to allow the flavours to develop. Stir in the garam masala and season to taste.

Serve with bowls of fresh coriander and chopped chillies, alongside warm rotis.

Gardener's Cottage Pie

A classic lentil and vegetable cottage pie with a golden topping of sweet potato and mature cheddar. The brown lentils give the pie body, whereas the red lentils help thicken the sauce.

1 cup (200 g) brown lentils
5 sweet potatoes, peeled and cubed
milk, for mashing
sea salt
freshly ground black pepper
1 Tbs (15 ml) butter
1 onion, finely sliced
2 carrots, peeled and diced
2 sticks celery, finely sliced
1 red chilli, finely sliced
2 Tbs (30 ml) olive oil
½ butternut, cubed
1 handful fresh parsley, finely
　chopped
1 bay leaf
1 cup (200 g) red lentils
1 tsp (5 ml) dried mixed herbs
6 cups (1.5 litres) vegetable stock,
　preferably homemade
1 x 410 g can chopped, peeled
　tomatoes
2 heaped Tbs (30 ml) tomato paste
grated cheddar, for sprinkling

S ERVES 6

Cook the brown lentils in a large pot of water for about 45 minutes, or until soft. (The red lentils have a much shorter cooking time and can be added directly to the sauce of the cottage pie during cooking.)

While the brown lentils are simmering, cook the sweet potatoes in boiling, salted water until soft. Mash the sweet potatoes, adding milk if necessary. Season, add a knob of butter and set aside.

Sauté the onion, carrots, celery and chilli in the olive oil until the onion is softened but not yet browned. Add the butternut, parsley, bay leaf, red lentils, dried herbs and stock. Bring to the boil and simmer, about 30 minutes, until the butternut and lentils are soft.

Add the tomatoes, tomato paste and cooked brown lentils, and bring back to a simmer. Turn off the heat.

Pour into a baking dish. Top with the mashed sweet potato, sprinkle with cheddar and bake in a preheated oven at 180 °C for 30 to 35 minutes, or until golden and bubbling.

Barley Risotto with Mushrooms and Parsley

A wholesome take on traditional risotto, barley lends a firmer texture and robust flavour. The combination of mushrooms, parsley and lemon zest makes for a very tasty dish.

6 cups (1.5 litres) vegetable stock,
  preferably homemade
1 onion, finely chopped
1 Tbs (30 g) butter
1 Tbs (15 ml) oil
1 cup (200 g) uncooked pearl barley
leaves from 6 thyme sprigs
180 g mixed mushrooms (I like to
  use oyster, shiitake and Portobello)
2 Tbs (60 g) butter
2 cloves garlic, finely chopped
6 Tbs (90 ml) dry white wine
1 handful parsley, finely chopped
juice and zest of 1 lemon
1 handful grated Parmesan
salt and black pepper, to taste

SERVES 6

Make sure that the stock is warm before you start making the risotto. If you add cold stock to the barley it will slow down the cooking process.

Sauté the onion in the butter and oil until translucent, but not yet browned. Add the barley, thyme and 2 cups (500 ml) of the warm stock. Bring to the boil, then simmer until most of the stock has been absorbed, stirring frequently for about 5 minutes.

Add the remaining stock, one ladle at a time, allowing the stock to be absorbed before adding the next ladle, until the barley is tender. Stir frequently. Cover and set aside.

In a clean saucepan, flash-fry the mushrooms in 2 tablespoons of butter over a high heat for about 2 minutes. Add the garlic, wine, parsley, lemon juice and zest. Turn down the heat and cook for about 3 minutes, or until the mushrooms are soft and most of the liquid has been absorbed or evaporated.

Add the mushrooms to the barley along with a knob of butter and a generous handful of Parmesan. Season and serve.

Black Rice Pudding with Condensed Milk

The colour of this comforting dessert is quite dramatic. Thai black rice makes an excellent rice pudding as the grains are naturally sweet and hold their shape well. Black rice also contains loads of fibre and antioxidants.

1 vanilla pod
2 cinnamon sticks
1 cup (200 g) black rice
3 cups (750 ml) water
¾ cup (190 ml) full cream milk
1–2 cans (385 g) sweetened
  condensed milk
ground cinnamon, to serve

SERVES 4

Cut the vanilla pod in half lengthwise and scrape out the seeds. Set the seeds aside and place the seedless vanilla pod, cinnamon sticks, rice and water in a pot and bring to the boil. Reduce to a simmer, then cover and cook for 45 minutes, by which time the rice should be cooked, but still slightly 'wet'. Remove the vanilla pod.

Add the milk, vanilla seeds and 1 can of the condensed milk to the rice (reserving the rest to serve) and, stirring slowly, bring to the boil. Reduce the heat and simmer uncovered for about 10 minutes, stirring occasionally. The rice should be beautifully creamy and thick, but with a fair amount of 'give'.

Cool to warm or room temperature, loosen with a little extra condensed milk if necessary, or some full cream milk if you prefer, and serve with a sprinkling of ground cinnamon.

Recipe Index

189

Thanks to ...

My mother, Marianne Palmer, and dear friends Leigh–Ann Matthews,
Brenda Wardall, Vicki Sleet and Margaret Matthews, for supplying props
Everyone at Café Roux for your time and space
My darling friend and style guru Lauren Marshall
Stan Hannath for the use of your vegetable garden and koekoeks
Jason Snell, Theo Lutz and Steve Botha for supplying fantastic produce
Franck Dangereux and Kerry Warren of The Foodbarn for 'borrowed goods'
Eric Bulpitt for the Jerusalem artichokes
The Pompous Fly and Pot Spot for props
Shannon Draper for the heirloom mielies and endless inspiration
Victoria Verbaan for bringing vegetables to life through the beautiful illustrations
Russel Wasserfall for the fun, laughs and highly skilled, professional work
Ceri Prenter for believing in me
Michelle Marlin and Marius Roux for bringing these pages to life
Paul for your constant love and support

SUNBIRD PUBLISHERS

First published in 2012

Sunbird Publishers (Pty) Ltd
The illustrated imprint of Jonathan Ball Publishers (Pty) Ltd
P O Box 6836,
Roggebaai 8012
Cape Town, South Africa

www.sunbirdpublishers.co.za

Registration number: 1984/003543/07

www.livetoeat.co.za

Design, typesetting and cover by MR Design
Photographs by Russel Wasserfall
Editing and project management by Michelle Marlin
Proofreading by Kathleen Sutton

Reproduction by Resolution Colour (Pty) Ltd, Cape Town
Printed and bound by Tien Wah Press (Pte) Ltd, Singapore

ISBN 978-1-920289-59-1

PREVIOUS PAGE: *Brandywine tomatoes*